INSIGHT COMPACT GUIDES

TURKISH COAST

Compact Guide: Turkish Coast is the ultimate quick-reference guide to this fascinating destination. It tells you everything you need to know about the region's attractions, contrasting the magic of ancient sites and cities with the bustle and colour of resorts and bazaars, the shimmering beauty of the coast with the rugged splendour of the hinterland.

This is just one title in *Apa Publications'* new series of pocket-sized, easy-to-use guidebooks intended for the independent-minded traveller. *Compact Guides* pride themselves on being up-to-date and authoritative. They are in essence mini travel encyclopedias, designed to be comprehensive yet portable, as well as readable and reliable.

GW00504099

Star Attractions

An instant reference
to some of the
Turkish Coast's most
popular tourist
attractions to help
you on your way.

Pergamon p23

Çeşme beach p32

Ephesus p35

Didyma p42

Bodrum bazaar p45

Marmaris p47

Antalya p55

Aspendos theatre p61

Xanthos p51

Alanya p65

Antakya p74

TURKISH Coast

Introduction

Places

Culture

Leisure

Practical Information

Turkish Coast – Sun, Sea and the Orient

The Turkish coast has many faces: miles of sandy beaches, idyllic bays, broad river valleys and an almost Alpine hinterland. Archaeologists have uncovered impressive Roman remains that testify to earlier greatness and links with Europe while, nearby, the ever-present mosques with their slim, towering minarets serve as a reminder that modern Turkish history has been influenced by Islam and the people still look to the east for their spiritual guidance. Five times a day the *muezzin* calls the faithful to prayer, the menfolk sit and chat in the coffee houses, exotic wares from the Orient are piled high in the bazaars and women wearing headscarves dominate the street scenes.

Carpets in Behramkale

On the other hand, the region stretching from İzmir to Adana in the Southeast ranks as one of the most progressive in Turkey. Modern air-conditioned hotels and office blocks are now common sights in the towns, the car has long since replaced the donkey and the camel, young men and women wear fashionable Western-style clothes. In recent years Turkey has turned more towards the west.

There is still much to see and to explore, almost too much for a two- to three-week holiday. Turkey has more sites of antiquity than Greece! Furthermore, the Turkish people greet holidaymakers with such warmth and exuberance. Take the opportunity offered by a Turkish holiday to get to know this unique and interesting culture and a new friendship is sure to emerge.

Antiquity at Pergamon

5

Situation and landscape

From Çanakkale by the Dardanelles, where a narrow channel of water separates Europe from Asia, the Turkish coast extends round to Antakya, a town that, from a geographical point of view, really belongs to Syria. While İzmir, the biggest town in the Mediterranean basin, lies on the same line of latitude as Sardinia, Antalya is level with Tunis. Thus Turkey connects Europe with Asia, and this bridging function has for centuries been an important element in the history of Asia Minor.

Geographically, the Turkish coast can be separated into two clearly defined regions. The west coast as far as Marmaris is characterised by bays, peninsulas reaching out into the Aegean and a hinterland dominated by broad, fertile river valleys and alluvial plains.

The region between Bergama (Pergamon) and Miletus, settled by Greeks until the end of World War I, was known in antiquity as Ionia and the coastal area to the north as Aeolia. Here lie the most important archaeological excavations from the Greek period. Around Bodrum and Marmaris, the

Young cotton picker

terrain becomes more mountainous and the foothills of the Taurus mountains overlook the sea. Between Fethiye and Antalya, the Taurus range extends down to the coast and Lycia, as it was called in antiquity, is still a difficult region to explore, although the construction of a new coast road in the 1980s has helped to open it up.

The south coast from Antalya eastwards has a more uniform character. Sometimes described as the 'Turkish Riviera', the coastline consists chiefly of long sandy beaches, which are backed by the fertile plain formerly known as Pamphylia. Further east lies ancient Cilicia and from Alanya to Anamur the landscape is wild and mountainous. This is where the Taurus mountains appear to emerge from the sea and where citrus fruits and bananas thrive. But then beyond Silifke the coastal strip broadens out into a vast plain around Adana where cotton and cereals flourish. Hatay province with the major cities of İskenderun and Antakya forms the final section of the Turkish coast.

Climate and when to go

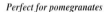
Perfect for pomegranates

A Mediterranean climate means hot, dry summers, wet winters and mild springs and autumns. However, the Turkish weather varies quite considerably from region to region, even in the coastal areas. Along the west coast, the Aegean north wind is an important influence and so the temperatures do not reach the same extremes as those of the south coast. The warmth of spring comes a little later and the cooler air of autumn will be felt rather earlier. From October onwards, visitors should come prepared for some unpleasant weather. The south coast, however, is protected from the north wind by the Taurus mountains and in summer the thermometer can reach 45°C (113°F) and even at night levels rarely fall below 30°C (86°F). The warm season starts here earlier and ends later. But in the southeast, in the Çukurova plain around Adana and in the province of Hatay, expect very high temperatures and high humidity. In summer a hot wind frequently blows across from the Syrian steppes.

Spring blossom

Spring is probably the best season for a visit to the Turkish coast. At this time of year the countryside is smothered in a carpet of blossom and, with temperatures hovering around 25°C (77°F), sea bathing is an inviting prospect. From the scenic point of view, Turkey is not at its best at the end of September, although by this time the temperatures will certainly have moderated. From June to September the sweltering heat is fine for bathers and beach-lovers but it can be debilitating and anyone with circulatory problems should avoid this time of year. Even in winter, the sun shines brightly and often, and the region between Antalya and Side is currently being marketed as a winter destination.

The Yayla

Today thousands of holidaymakers flock to the Turkish beaches in the summer, but long before the advent of tourism the semi-nomadic village farmers decided to keep well away from the coast at this time of year. They packed up their belongings and headed for the cool Yayla, the high plains of the Taurus range, where a pleasant 20°C (68°F) is normal for summer. Here it was possible to reap a second harvest, while the vegetation in the lower plains burned beneath a baking hot sun. Now few farmers make the trek into the mountains for the summer months, although it is still popular among Turkish picnickers. The upper plains also make good walking country.

Flora and fauna

The fauna and flora along the coast are almost subtropical in character and many visitors will encounter species that they have never seen before.

Land that is not used for agricultural purposes can be divided into two types. Along the coast, the vegetation has adapted to the long, dry summers: kermes oaks, cork oaks, strawberry trees, laurels and thorny bushes create a low-growing scrub. In spring an impressive mass of colour carpets the inhospitable terrain, but the blossom is short-lived. Elsewhere the fruits of the palm, fig, almond and carob trees are harvested.

At higher altitudes, cedars of Lebanon grow alongside fir and spruce forests.

If they have not already disappeared, the habitats of many animal species are seriously threatened by the growth of the towns, the increasing demand for farmland and the modernisation of farming methods. The destruction of the natural environment is as much of a problem in Turkey as it is anywhere else in the developing world. Since the end of the 1980s, the government has given some

Beachgoers near Çeşme

Farm produce

7

Melons galore

A contented flock

Camel encounter
Goat among the ruins

regions protected status, but with limited success to date. As a consequence of land speculation, concrete now covers large expanses of the coastal region.

Nevertheless, the metallic-looking skin of the star lizard can still be seen gleaming in the sun on quiet rocks, although snakes are rare. Stork hunting, once very common in Turkey, is now banned, but the bird's numbers continue to fall. The Taurus mountains are rich in wildlife with foxes, badgers and lynx still plentiful, as are buzzards, kites and falcons. Bears used to roam the uplands but today visitors will only see the dancing bears used to entertain town dwellers. Camels can still be encountered, but again, only as tourist attractions. Donkeys and beasts of burden no longer have useful jobs to do, but flocks of sheep and goats can often be seen clambering over the Greek and Roman ruins. Water buffalo are used as working animals in the southeast.

Dalyan and Iztuzu beach (*see Route 4, page 48*) have come to represent a reconciliation between tourism and environmental protection. In 1987, plans for a huge hotel complex to be paid for by German financiers threatened the existence of the loggerhead turtle (*caretta caretta*), as it was around these shores that the female laid her eggs. Turkish environmentalists brought the matter to the public's attention. The German government became involved and they eventually withdrew their support for the scheme. Instead there are now just a few small pensions, and some wooden kiosks, and the authorities agreed to ban bathing at the southeast end of the beach. Meanwhile, however, all the publicity that the campaign spawned led to a new type of tourism, 'ecotourism', which brought another new source of disturbance for the turtles. Be that as it may, the Dalyan story can still be considered a major victory for conservation.

Population and religion

With a population of around 40 million, the Turkish coast is home to about two thirds of the population of Turkey (62.5m). İzmir (2.1m) and Adana (1.1m) are the main centres of population, while Antalya, Antakya and Mersin are also major cities. During the summer the population along the coast is swelled by thousands of seasonal workers who find employment in the tourist industry and also on the farms helping with the harvest.

Modesty prevails

Asia Minor, for centuries a melting pot of many different races and cultures, is now inhabited predominantly by Turks. The many different ethnic groups – so characteristic of the Turkey of the Ottoman empire which survived until shortly after World War I – have, as a result of a rigid policy of assimilation, now almost disappeared. Large Greek communities lived alongside the Turks in İzmir and in many of the villages on the west and south coasts, but in 1923 they were forcibly repatriated to their 'motherland'. Armenians, a large minority in the area around Adana, were also expelled in the chaos following World War I. The full story of their departure makes a sorry chapter in Turkish history.

While many of the other peoples who settled in Turkey during the Ottoman years, arriving from such places as the Balkans, Syria, Libya and Yemen, have now lost their cultural identities, the Kurds have resisted the trend towards assimilation. They have retained their own culture, continuing to speak a language similar to Persian, and the refusal of Turkish politicians to grant special privileges to this minority has led to an escalation of racial conflict in the southeastern corner of the country. The Kurdish issue remains the most serious political problem facing the government in Ankara.

Very few religious minorities now live in Turkey. There are a few Greek Orthodox Christians and Jews in İstanbul, a small Jewish community lives in Çanakkale and about 20,000 Christians of the Syrian Orthodox faith reside in Hatay province. Some 98 percent of all Turks are Moslems and Islam, in all its many manifestations, plays an important part in private and public life. Five times a day the *muezzin* calls the faithful to prayer, during Ramadan, the month of fasting, cafés and tea houses remain empty (but stay open in the tourist areas) and at the fountains outside the mosques, men wash themselves in accordance with Islamic tradition before attending Friday prayers. On the other hand, the Turkish constitution declares that following the teachings of Islam is a private matter and the intolerance shown to those who do not conform, seen in other countries of the Middle East, is not evident in Turkey, even though activists have recently started calling for a return to the old ways.

9

Prayer time in Adana

Islam (meaning devotion to God) is a strictly monotheistic religion. It was founded by Mohammed, a prophet in the same tradition as Moses and Jesus, who found God (Allah) through the Archangel Gabriel. Islam is like Christianity in that the teachings are given in a book, the collected words of Mohammed. These sacred texts are known as the Koran (sermon) and are written in the flowery language typical of the Arab world. The Koran contains God's word, already revealed to the Jews, on how man should submit to his will. It also lays down the moral code by which all believers should live. The five main duties of all Moslems, the so-called Five Pillars of Islam, are the profession of faith, daily prayer, the duty to give alms, fasting at Ramadan and the pilgrimage to Mecca.

From an historical perspective, Islam represents the basis for the huge expansion of the Arab world which extends as far as the south of France. Even the Turkic tribes, who adopted Islam in about AD800, conquered Asia Minor as part of a holy war. The advance of the Ottoman empire to become a world power took place under the green flag of the prophet.

Islam, a religion which has never had an official mouthpiece like the Catholic church in Rome, is interpreted in many different ways depending largely on the extent of the believer's education and background. There has, however, been a doctrinal split in the teachings of Islam. Sunni Moslems base their beliefs on the words and deeds of the prophet Mohammed but there are also four different schools of law. Shiites, on the other hand, follow the spiritual leadership of the daughter and son-in-law of the prophet. Most Turks are Sunnis and follow the moderate Hanefitic law school. Between about a fifth and a third of all Turks regard themselves as Alevites, who interpret the Koran as Shias but generally are more liberal.

The mosque

In modern Turkey mosques are enjoying a new lease of life. They are springing up at about the same rate as fitness centres in western Europe. Huge concrete domes and slim minarets soar above the rooftops in the tiniest of villages, but this development has little to do with the rise of fundamentalism and much more to do with the increasing number of wealthy Turks. For Moslems, endowing a mosque is seen as an act of great piety.

The new Grand Mosque in Adana

Larger mosques are called *cami* and they are used principally for the communal Friday prayer session and address. The smaller *mesçit*, on the other hand, is a room for prayer. A *cami* usually has a forecourt *(haram)* with a washing fountain *(şadırvan)* for the ritual ablution ceremony that must be undertaken before prayers. A niche *(mihrab)* in the prayer room marks the direction of Mecca *(kibla)*. The chancel *(mimber)* from where the priest *(imam)* conducts Friday prayers is situated alongside the niche. A mosque often stands amid a number of other buildings such as the *medrese* (Koran school), *hastane* (hospital), *imaret* (almshouse) and *türbele* (mausolea) built to honour the mosque's founders. All visitors to mosques must remove their footwear before entering.

An older edifice in İzmir

11

Language

Turkish is a relatively difficult language to learn, but English is widely spoken particularly in the major centres. It may, however, be worthwhile taking the trouble to learn a few pronunciation rules so that at least streets and place-names can be correctly pronounced.

- **c:** *dj* as in 'John', eg cadde (street) = *djadde*.
- **ç:** *ch* as in 'church', eg çay (tea) = *chai*.
- **ğ:** is not spoken. It simply lengthens the preceding vowel, eg Samandağ = *samandaa*.
- **h:** clearly sounded like the *-ch* of 'loch', eg kahvalte (breakfast) = *kachvalte*.
- **ı:** (dotless i) sounds like the *-er* in 'mother', eg kapı (gate) = *kape*.
- **j:** like the *s* in pleasure, eg plaj (beach) = *plaazh*.
- **s:** unvoiced as in 'yes', eg sabun (soap).
- **Ş:** *sh* as in 'shame', eg Şeker (sugar) = *shaker*.
- **Z:** voiced s as in 'rose', eg güzel (beautiful) = *goozel*.

Economy

The Turkish Mediterranean coast is one of Turkey's most prosperous regions. From an agricultural point of view, the soil is the most fertile and, with artificial irrigation, as many as three harvests per year can be achieved. The lines of greenhouses for fruit and vegetables extend for miles. But industry is also well established here with the

Cotton bales near İzmir

three free-trade zones of İzmir, Antalya and Mersin reaping the benefit. Cotton and the export-oriented textile industry have played an important part in the region's revival too. High levels of government investment have improved the transport and urban infrastructure and speculators have also moved in to build new hotels and private homes. The coastal strip now attracts tens of thousands of seasonal workers every year. Tourism has become the region's most important industry and many Turks now earn their living from meeting the needs of the holidaymakers, having left the plains of central Anatolia probably for good.

The waterfront in Alanya

12

Turkish carpets

Turkish knotted-pile carpets *(halı)* and *kilims* go back to the ancient traditions of the Turkman nomads of central Asia and must now rank as one of Turkey's most successful exports. Genuine carpets or *kilims* are hand-made, almost always by women. Central Anatolia is the main production source but carpet weaving also goes on by the coast. Factories welcome visitors and the staff are generally to happy to explain the techniques used.

Every knot is tied individually. On a good quality carpet, each square centimetre will have 42 knots (6 x 7), that is 420,000 knots per square metre. A significant feature of the Turkish carpet is the *gördes* knot. A woollen strand is looped around a double warp thread to create a firm, long pile but with much coarser patterns than those of the finer Persian *sineh* knots. The pattern on the prayer carpet or *seccade* is principally a stylised prayer niche, while the larger floor carpets usually have geometric or floral patterns. The flat-woven *kilims* fall into two categories: *barak kilims* and the more tightly-woven *sumak kilims*. They are both more functional and the pattern styles are more varied.

A choice of designs in Didyma

Carpet patterns have undergone a number of changes over the centuries. The earliest Turkish carpets displayed Chinese motifs, but animals started to appear under the Seljuks. Ottoman carpet-weavers preferred floral patterns in the Persian style and these remain the favourites today, although carpets in 'pop-art' style abound.

Anyone wishing to buy a Turkish carpet should carry out a quick market survey. Complaints are rife about fake silk carpets, old carpets which have been trimmed, and extortionate prices. The threads used for the knots should be wool. One way of checking the material is to apply the burn test. Cotton burns without a smell, but there is no mistaking the smell of burning wool.

Government and politics

Flag waving and vote catching

Turkey is a centralised state, divided up into 72 provinces, each run by a government-appointed administrator. At the moment martial law applies in 10 of the southeastern provinces. In the towns, elected representatives enjoy a degree of autonomy. The head of state (currently Süleyman Demirel) appoints the prime minister. The present one, Tansu Çiller, leads a coalition government comprising the DYP, a middle-class conservative party of which she is the leader, and the social democratic SHP. The ANAP (Motherland Party) held the reins of power for much of the 1980s under the leadership of Turgut Özal but his party was banished to the opposition benches in 1991. ANAP's principal policy successes, namely the liberalisation of the economy and the expansion of tourism and exports, are supported by the present government.

In July 1995, with the overwhelming support of MPs, Mrs Çiller succeeded in steering through parliament 16 amendments to Turkey's military-era constitution. This democratisation package, which included allowing students and academics to join political parties and civil servants to form trades unions, was welcomed across Turkey, although it did not receive the support of the fundamentalist Islamic Welfare (Refah) Party, which made such substantial and sensational gains in the municipal elections held during 1994.

In 1995 there were moves to devolve power from the capital to local authorities, a development which many analysts believe will be a giant step towards ending the war for self-rule in the mainly Kurdish southeast. Meanwhile, Mrs Çiller is staking her political future on continued improvements in economic performance and the customs union between Turkey and the European Union. Acutely aware of Turkey's poor record on human rights, the government has also been fighting to change the notorious anti-terror law, and to safeguard freedom of thought and freedom of speech.

Historical Highlights

Around 150,000 years old Bones from a relative of Neanderthal man have been found in the Karain caves near Antalya.

3rd millennium BC Regional principalities such as Troy in the Aegean are founded.

1800–1200BC Eastern and central Anatolia are ruled by Hittites, while the Aegean is influenced by Minoan, later Mycenean culture.

9th–6th century BC Greeks settle on the west and south coasts of Asia Minor. Carians, Lycians, Phrygians and Lydians carve out territories along the Aegean coast.

546BC The Lydian empire and the Greek cities in western Asia Minor are conquered by the Persians.

494BC The Ionian cities on the west coast rise vainly against the Persians. Miletus and Priene are destroyed.

334BC Alexander the Great begins his conquest of Asia Minor and the Persian empire. The Diadochs (Macedonian generals) take over the empire on his death in Babylon in 323.

282BC The Pergamene empire is founded.

190BC The Romans defeat Antiochus III at Magnesia (modern Manisa) and impose their rule over Asia Minor.

133BC The Pergamene empire falls to the Romans. It opts to become a province of Rome.

20BC Pax Romana, the peace treaty with the Parthian Persians, initiates a period of peace lasting 200 years.

AD330 Emperor Constantine moves the capital of the Roman empire to Byzantium on the Bosphorus (now İstanbul). Asia Minor is at the heart of the Roman empire.

395 The Emperor Theodosius divides the Roman Empire between his sons. Asia Minor is now the heart of the Byzantine Empire, which comprises the entire eastern Mediterranean.

638 Arabs capture Antioch and attack the coast of Asia Minor.

1071 Seljuks defeat the Byzantines in eastern Anatolia and push westward.

1204 Knights of the Fourth Crusade conquer Constantinople.

1243 The Seljuks are defeated by Mongols and the Seljuk rulers are forced to become vassals of the Mongol invaders. Asia Minor remains under the control of Turkic tribes.

1288 Osman I, leader of a Turkic tribe, lays the foundations for the Ottoman empire.

1453 Constantinople captured and fortified by the Ottomans.

1512–20 Selim I subjugates Persia and Egypt. All of Asia Minor falls under Ottoman rule.

1520–66 Selim's son, Suleyman the Magnificent, comes close to capturing Vienna (1529). The Ottoman empire is at its most powerful.

1770 Turkish fleet destroyed by the Russians at Çeşme.

1821–30 Greek War of Independence. The Ottomans lose the Peloponnese and central Greece. Turkish control over the Balkans and north Africa weakens.

1908 Young Turks revolution.

1914–18 Turkey enters World War I in support of the Germans, but the army eventually collapses. The country is occupied by allied troops and divided up into zones of occupation.

1919 Mustafa Kemal, later Atatürk (*see page 15*), organises resistance to the occupation.

1921–3 Greek–Turkish war. All Greeks in Asia Minor are repatriated.

1923 The Turkish Republic is proclaimed with Ankara as its capital. Mustafa Kemal is declared president.

1925–38 Period of reforms in which Mustafa Kemal seeks to create a modern, Western-style state.

1938 Atatürk dies and İsmet İnönü becomes president.

1939–45 Turkey remains neutral during World War II.

1960, 1971, 1980 Military intervention in government.

1974 Turkey invades northern Cyprus.

1982 New constitution. General Kenan Evren becomes president.

1983 Free elections. Turgut Özal becomes prime minister and starts programme of economic reforms.

1989 Özal becomes president.

1991 Süleyman Demirel (DYP) leads a centre-left coalition government.

1993 Özal dies and Demirel becomes president. Tansu Çiller, the first Turkish woman to hold high office, leads the coalition government.

1994 Kurdish guerillas in conflict with Turkish army in southwest Anatolia. Islamic Welfare Party makes huge gains in municipal elections.

1995 Çiller's government embarks on a programme of amendments to the military-era constitution, ushering in a new period of democratisation. Moves to devolve power from the capital to local authorities.

Atatürk

Atatürk is ever-present in Turkey – on postcards, busts and statues, wall plates, carpets, even sketched with stones on a mountain side. The army leader, statesman, thinker, friend of the people looks down from the classroom wall and reading primers tell of his heroic words and deeds. No other 20th-century leader has achieved the same lasting dominance over his or her people.

Born in Salonica in 1881, he acquitted himself well in military campaigns before and during World War I. He worked his way up the military hierarchy to become a general and after defeat in 1918, he started to organise a popular resistance movement against both the Allies and the rule of the sultans. In 1923 he founded the Turkish Republic and was elected to become president of the Turkish National Assembly – an office that he held until his death in 1938.

Mustafa Kemal was always a radical 'Westerniser'. At that time, the world was still ruled from western Europe's capitals, so it is understandable that a man who read European literature, liked drinking *rakı*, enjoyed the company of attractive women, wore elegant suits and drove smart cars would believe that the adoption of Western values and customs was the best way to achieve economic progress.

The population was obliged to break with many old habits: Western dress was permitted, the use of the Arabic alphabet was banned, the holy law of Islam, the *sharia*, was replaced by a legal system based on the western model. He reformed the calendar, banned mystic religious orders and closed the monasteries. Whether to follow the precepts of the Islamic faith or not became a matter for the individual. That the resurrection of the 'sick man by the Bosphorus' aroused worldwide admiration is due chiefly to the charismatic appeal and skills of Mustafa Kemal and he was later awarded the title of Atatürk (father of the Turks) by the National Assembly.

The Dardanelles

War and death have been ever-present beside these 65-km (40-mile) long straits which separate two continents – at their narrowest point east and west are no more than 1.3km (¾ miles) apart. It was here that the Persian king Xerxes set out for Europe and Alexander the Great crossed to Asia. There are legends which pay tribute to the mysterious forces at work in this sea channel. A famous love story ended tragically in the Dardanelles when young Leander drowned in a storm as he set out to cross the channel on one of his nocturnal visits to Hero, who was a priestess of Aphrodite.

During World War I the Dardanelles were the scene of carnage. Ottoman forces had blocked the waterway, but the Allies, who needed to supply Russian troops, tried to force their way through. In April 1915 the Allies, principally Commonwealth troops, tried, under deadly fire from Turkish coastal batteries, to reach the heights on the European side of the Dardanelles so that they could exercise full control over the seaway. Both sides suffered terrible losses, but the battle was a serious setback for the Allies.

Cosmopolitan Çanakkale
Preceding pages: Knidos

Route 1

Troas and the land of Homer

Çanakkale to İzmir via Troy and Bergama (332km/205 miles) *See map on page 20*

Start in Europe, cross over the Dardanelles, the famous channel that separates the continents (*see page 15*), and arrive twenty minutes later in Asia. It is possible to be in İzmir (*see page 28*) on the same day, but slow down! The route south passes via Troy, the ruins immortalised in Homer's *Iliad* and then runs through the uplands of the Troas, still largely undeveloped as a tourist region, down to the sea. Beach follows beach interspersed with broad olive groves. Ayvalık, formerly a Greek town, is particularly picturesque, as is Bergama – known in antiquity as Pergamon – a town which offers much more than monuments to its illustrious past. Continue south through plains and fertile upland, past ancient shrines and forgotten towns such as Kyme and secluded resorts like Çandarlı, Bademli or Yeni Foça. Allow at least two days for the journey to İzmir, a city much more representative of the real Turkey than any tourist resort.

Çanakkale couple

Çanakkale (pop. 75,000) was known as **Kale-i-Sultaniye** (Sultan's Castle) until it became an important pottery-producing town in the 18th century. It was then renamed Çanakkale meaning 'Pot Castle'. The older name does make sense as the Ottomans built four castles near or over-looking the Dardanelles in order to maintain control over this strategically important channel. Together with the clover-leaf complex of ★ **Kilitbahir** on the European side, the Kale-i-Sultaniye (1452), which now houses a military

Military museum

museum, is the main sight of historic interest in the town. To experience the appeal of a small Turkish town, savour the atmosphere outside the reasonably-priced *lokantalar* by the clock tower. The ★ **Archaeological Museum** (Tuesday to Sunday 9am–noon and 1–5pm) on the edge of the town is not to be missed. As well as some remarkable Ionian grave stelae, exhibits include jewellery that was discovered in the nearby Dardanos tumulus (4th century BC) and finds from the most recent excavations at the ancient city of Troy.

Archaeological Museum

Troy

Troy is a protected zone

The world-famous ruined site of ★★ **Troy** (Turkish = Truva; daily 8am–7pm) is situated near the village of Tevfikiye on Hisarlık Hill. It is now designated as an archaeological protected zone.

There are a number of restaurants by the entrance and also the medium category **Bozdir** hotel, while Tevfikiye itself can only offer basic private accommodation and the **Karol** pension. The modestly-furnished **Schliemann House** by the approach road testifies to the self-discipline of the German archaeologist who spent many years of considerable hardship here.

Antiquity unearthed

Heinrich Schliemann (1822–90) was a successful German businessman who used his fortune to fulfil a dream. Having read Homer as a child, he took the author at his word and used his own determination and judgement to triumph over the cynicism of experts who were not inclined to take a self-taught man seriously. Right up to his death, Schliemann excavated the walls and palaces of Homer's Troy. In June 1873 he even uncovered what he believed was the 'Treasure of Priam'. Priam was the father of Paris who abducted Helen, the event which is said to have provoked the Trojan War.

The Troy that Schliemann believed was burnt down by the Greeks turned out, after later excavation work, to be a thousand years older than the Troy described in Homer's *Iliad* and this fact has cast doubt on the historical accuracy of the Homeric legend. The *Iliad* recounts how the Greek warriors of Agamemnon waged war for 10 years but were finally defeated by the guile of Odysseus. It is not really an account of a modern war but deals rather with a confrontation between the Greeks and the peoples of Asia Minor. Whether this battle was squeezed into one particular place, whether this place was Hisarlık Hill and whether Schliemann really discovered Homer's Troy remain unanswered questions.

The only thing that is certain is that Hisarlık Hill has been inhabited almost without a break from the beginning of the Iron Age. The numerous finds have enabled archaeologists to piece together the early history of west-

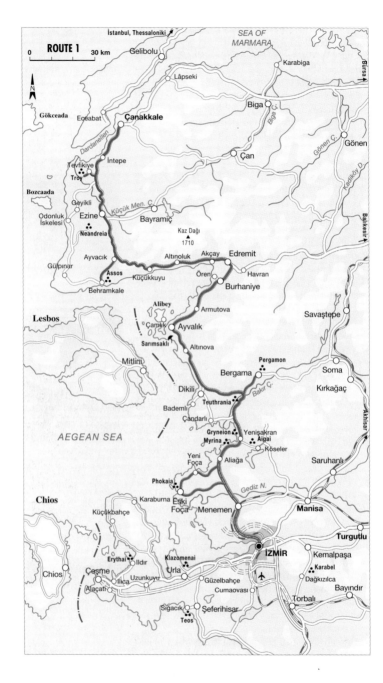

ern Anatolia. Excavations are continuing, but work on most of the lower town at the foot of the settlement hill has already been completed.

The 10 periods of settlement date from about 3700BC (Troy 0) to AD400 (Troy IX). For those who give credence to the *Iliad* story and Schliemann's interpretation, Homeric Troy is linked either with Troy VI or VII, but these settlements were destroyed in the 13th or 12th century BC and there is no hint of any Greek influence. A tour of Troy is rather like visiting a museum: many areas are roped off.

Amongst the ruins

The signposted footpath leads first to the **town ramparts** of Troy VI (1900–1300BC). It is sloping and broken up by strips of wall. A section of Roman **foundations** with a vertical drop (on the right) clearly indicates the structural differences. A modern flight of steps which replaces a Late Bronze Age ramp leads up past four dwellings that date from Troy VI and VII.

The **acropolis** offers a fine view over the site and also contains an interesting Roman **well shaft**. A **bastion** (Troy VI) strengthened the fortifications for the mound and also protected a cistern (not accessible).

The **Temple of Athena** was built by the emperor Augustus and replaced a shrine from the Hellenistic era. In the courtyard area a number of stone blocks that formed part of the substructure have survived. None of the stones for the temple remain in place, although grooved column drums, the remains of Doric entablatures and fragments of a marble coffered ceiling lie scattered around. The footpath now carries on to Troy's oldest settlement level and one which is currently enjoying the attention of archaeologists. The newly-uncovered burnt layer dates from around 3700BC.

21

Perhaps the most impressive sight of all is the **Bronze Age ramp** from Troy II (2500–2150BC). It measures 21m (68ft) in length and 5.5m (18ft) in width and pierces the loam walls of the second town. The famous 'Treasure of Priam', the ultimate prize for Schliemann, was uncovered about 20m (65ft) to the northwest. Immediately to the east of the ramp stands the **magazine**, a large structure that dates from Troy VI.

The Bronze Age ramp

The sacred area on the other side of the old town wall consisting of several altars and sacrificial fountains dates originally from Hellenistic times but was modified by the Romans. To the west, at the foot of the hill, lie two other **Roman buildings**: an **odeion** for musical performances and the **bouleuterion** or town hall. Both are set out like theatres with rising rows of seats.

The odeion

The south gate of Troy VI and the generously proportioned **Pillar House** (26 x 12m/85 x 40ft) can only be viewed from a distance. The **museum** at the end of the tour contains a number of modest finds, mainly pottery.

Ayvacık

Carpet seller in Behramkale

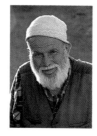

Temple of Athena and acropolis

The coastal motorway continues south to **Ezine** (50km/31 miles; pop 12,000), a rather impoverished little town with a number of modest hotels. Only those travellers interested in the remote ruined sites of **Neandria** and **Alexandreia Troas** or the island of **Bozcaada** (ferries from Odun İskelesi), will wish to stop off here.

Ayvacık (75km/46 miles; pop. 4,000) with its pretty town centre lies further on beyond magnificent pine forests. At the co-operatively run carpet school by the entrance to the town, it is possible to study the old knotting techniques and also find some bargains. Remains of the ancient town of Assos can be found in the picturesque village of **Behramkale** (19km/12 miles; beware! winding road). Have a break in the town before making a tour of the historic settlement.

★ **Assos** is spread out over a hill (235m/770ft) above the Aegean and the splendid view encompasses the Greek island of Lesbos. In the 9th or 8th century BC, Aeolian Greeks took over this hillside settlement from Asia Minor tribesmen. During the 4th century BC at the age of 37 the philosopher Aristotle played a part in the town's cultural ascent by founding the Assos School of Philosophy. Christianity gained a foothold early on, probably as a result of direct contact with the apostles Paul and Luke who both visited Troas. The decline of Assos began in the 3rd century AD, culminating in 1403 when the Mongol Timur plundered the town.

Much of interest remains. In Behramkale itself there is an Ottoman **humpback bridge** that was used by the caravans as they carried their loads from the harbour towards the Dardanelles and also a 14th-century **mosque**. On the slopes above the village some Byzantine **towers** and a vaulted cistern are visible. Up on the hill, the principal sight is the **Temple of Athena**, the only Doric temple in

Asia Minor. It was built about 530BC. On the southern slopes stands the Hellenistic agora complex which includes a stoa, market place, gymnasium and town hall. The sparse remains of some Roman **baths** and a **theatre** auditorium minus its seats are visible a little lower down.

Also included in a tour of Assos should be the **town wall**, with the section on the west side of the hill probably the best preserved. By the west gate, take a quick look at the **mausolea** and **sarcophagi** before following the cobbled path to the harbour. A number of hotels, restaurants and camp-sites overlook the narrow beach. A much bigger beach, albeit with very little shade, is to be found at the small resort of **Kadırga**, 4km (2½ miles) further east.

Bay of Edremit

The west coast motorway snakes its way east from Ayvacık with motorists being treated to some superb views over the sea and down 300m (1,000ft) to the **Bay of Edremit**. **Küçükkuyu** is the first in a series of busy resorts in the bay. Others include **Altınoluk**, **Akçay** and **Ören**. The latter is set amid pine woods and is probably the prettiest.

★ **Ayvalık** (175km/109 miles) offers a complete contrast. It is still obvious from the buildings that this was once a Greek town. **Taksiyarhis Kilise** in the town centre is worth a visit. Inside this 19th-century Greek Orthodox church are some unusual stencilled paintings. Also worth noting are the high **portals** to the houses. The town successfully combines the role of a modern resort, where the lively beaches, discos and night cruises attract many visitors, with the traditional lifestyle of the olive farmers, which continues in the town centre. Ayvalık also lies in the heart of a pleasant coastal landscape and is a centre for visitors to the two dozen or so offshore islands and the sandy beaches on the Sarımsaklı and Alibey peninsulas.

A family outing

One popular destination is **Şeytan Sofrası**, a fissure at the west end of Sarımsaklı beach. Throw a coin into the cleft in the rock and a wish will come true!

Bergama/Pergamon

★★ Bergama (225km/139 miles; pop. 60,000) is much more than just a backdrop for impressive ancient ruins. With its traditional bazaar, where visitors can admire the skills of shoemakers, tailors, barbers and brassworkers, examine the exotic wares on sale in the grocery stalls, be charmed by enthusiastic carpet salesmen or just relax in one of the many tea rooms or simple restaurants, Bergama is the real Turkey. And yet above the frenzied bustle of the narrow alleys – especially busy on Monday, the market day – the citadel is always visible, serving as a reminder of the town's distinguished past.

Bargains at Bergama's bazaar

Turkish baths in Bergama

The fertility of the two river valleys, the Bergama and Kestel Çayi, – known in antiquity as Selinus and Ketios, the proximity of the sea and the protection offered by the citadel contributed to the importance of the settlement, where at the beginning of the 3rd century BC Lysimachos, a general in Alexander the Great's army, entrusted the eunuch Philetairos with the enormous sum of 9,000 talents. After Lysimachos died, Philetairos declared the city independent and, when he handed over power to his nephew Eumenes, created a kingdom that stretched along the northern Aegean coast. He formed an alliance with the Romans and elevated Pergamon to one of the leading powers in Asia Minor. Eumenes and Attalos became important patrons of the arts and the many grand buildings and the famous library which was reputed to contain 200,000 volumes testify to their enormous wealth and benevolence.

In Egyptian Alexandria, the cultural centre of the ancient world, manuscripts were written on papyrus, while in Asia Minor wafer-thin animal skins were used, ie parchment, a word which is derived from Pergamon, where this material was first made. It was the city's close links with Rome which led eventually to the last Attalid rulers surrendering the city to the Roman empire. The Romans used Pergamon as a territorial base and their presence granted western Asia Minor a period of peaceful prosperity which ended with attacks by the Goths in the 3rd century AD. Under Byzantine rule new walls were built around the citadel to repel Arab intruders. When the Seljuks seized Pergamon in 1302, Bergama, as Pergamon was now called, moved from the hilltop to the plain below.

Pergamon has commanding views

In 1869 the German engineer Carl Humann (1839–96) took lodgings in Bergama where he was engaged on a road-building contract. He later discovered that chalk-burners were using fragments of rock that they had found on the citadel and he could not help noticing that these fragments had once been part of a high-quality frieze. He acquired some of the slabs, sent them back to the Berlin Museum and in 1878 systematic excavations began on the site where Humann and his team uncovered one of the masterpieces of Hellenism, the **Pergamon Altar**. The German engineer was granted special permission by the sultan to dismantle the altar, stone by stone, and to ship it from the port of Dikili back to Berlin, where a special room was built for it in what is now the Pergamon Museum. For many years now, Bergama has been calling for the return of this magnificent work of art.

From an art historian's point of view, the two friezes are the most remarkable features of the altar: on the inner side of the colonnade which surrounds the sacrificial altar, the mythical story of the founder of Pergamon, Telephos,

The altar is now in Berlin

is told, while on the outer frieze (120m x 2.3m/390 x 7.5ft) the gods are portrayed battling against the Gigantes. The deities fight on that side of the altar which corresponds to their nature. Poseidon, Nereus and Oceanus, for example, are on the west, ie the sea-facing side, while on the shady north side the god of the night, Nyx, and the goddess of strife, Eris, are shown. The sun god Helios is seen on the south side riding ahead of Eos, the goddess of the dawn, while on the east side, the goddess of victory, Nike, Apollo, Artemis and the only mortal, the strongman Hercules, are gathered around Zeus and Athena. The battle scenes are skilfully broken up but it is the vivid depiction of the action that is the most impressive aspect of the whole outer frieze: the figures, impassioned and agitated, almost stand clear of the background.

Frieze detail, Berlin

The best way to approach the citadel is from below. The starting point for a tour of the site is the **lower agora [A]** (follow the blue markings). Continue along a peaceful Byzantine cobbled road and through the ruined splendour of the three **gymnasiums [B]**, one for boys, one for adolescents and one for young men. The baths, toilets, basement stadium, room of honour and an odeion, for musical performances, were all part of the gymnasium complex. Lizards bask on the rocks absorbing the sun and the warmth radiating from the marble. The **Sanctuary of Demeter [C]** is followed by the foundations of the residential town and then an ancient pavement leads to the site of the Pergamon Altar and the much-visited upper town.

Temple of Trajan

25

This part of the tour usually begins on the ★★ **acropolis** situated by the car park on the citadel. The main monuments of antiquity are huddled together to the west. Not everything is as grand as it once was. Little remains of the famous **library [D]** and not much of the **Sanctuary of Athena** either. The ruins of the **Kings' Palaces [E]** and the **arsenals** right at the top are unimpressive but at least there is a wide-ranging view from the 335-m (1,098-ft) summit.

Not all of the ancient buildings have been lost. The ★★ **Temple of Trajan [F]** has been partially rebuilt. The Roman emperor Trajan (AD98–117) was especially keen on furthering the interests of Asia Minor and in AD112, Pergamene masons started work on the temple but it was not finished until 129 when Hadrian was emperor. This monumental structure 70m x 65m (230 x 212ft), a showpiece of Roman power and wealth, stands on a platform above a colonnaded terrace.

The second principal sight can be reached via a narrow flight of steps which leads from a Byzantine tower at the west end of the courtyard around

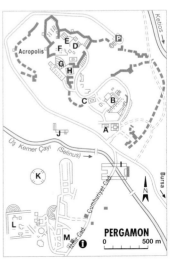

PERGAMON
0   500 m

26

the Shrine of Athena: the ★★ **theatre [G]** dates from the 3rd century BC. The 80 rows of seats could accommodate over 10,000 spectators and those at the back were 37m (120ft) above the stage which extended both to the left and right on to the **theatre terrace**. At the north end of the terrace stood the **Temple of Dionysos**.

The **Pergamon Altar [H]**, an even more famous shrine, dedicated to Zeus, would occupy pride of place today, had it not been removed. Now only five steps of the substructure remain. Built between 180 and 170BC it enclosed an area 36 x 34m (118 x 111ft).

There is still much to see at a lower level. With the security provided by the Roman empire the town was able to expand on to the plain where Bergama now stands. The ★ **Red Basilica [I]** (Kızıl Avlu) was built in the early 2nd century AD. It was originally a marble-clad brick structure, 19m (62ft) high and fronted by a courtyard that spanned the Selinus river (now Üş Kemer Çayi). This holy site was used to worship the Egyptian trio of gods, Serapis, Isis and Harpokrates, but in Christian times the temple was converted into a church. Nearby stands Bergama's 14th-century **Ulu Cami** or Great Mosque **[J]**.

Anyone wishing to view the impressive ruins of the ★ **amphitheatre [K]**, another *grand projet* from the Roman years, will have to venture into Bergama's poor quarter. However, strangers are not always welcomed by the local children who sometimes show their hostility by throwing stones. At one time the stream that flows in the theatre grounds was dammed up so that gladiators could enact sea battles on water.

The only other ruined site away from the citadel is the ★ **Asklepieion [L]**. The name derives from the Greek hero Asklepios, who was revered as the god of healing. From the 4th century BC until well into the Roman era invalids came here for dream interpretation and for treatment with both water and mud. The ★★ **Shrine of Asklepios** comprised a temple, a treatment room (both mid-2nd century BC), a Roman theatre, a library in honour of the emperor Hadrian and colonnades. A tunnel, which has survived over 2,000 years, leads from the treatment room to the sacred well.

In the ★ **Archaeological Museum [M]** on Bergama's main street (Cumhuriyet Cad: Tuesday to Sunday 7am–5pm), it is possible to review the glorious past of this once great city.

Return to the motorway and continue south to İzmir. A detour through the **Bakır Çayı** delta to the attractively sited coastal village of **Çandarli** (35km/22 miles from Bergama; pop. 2,500) is worthwhile. Situated close to the ancient Greek port of Pitane, its principal sight is a Genoese

castle that was built at the end of the 13th century, and to the northwest lies a good sandy beach (with some basic family pensions, and restaurants).

The harbour at Yeni Foça

The ancient sites of **Elaia, Myrina, Gryneion, Kyme** and **Larisa** further south may interest the amateur archaeologist but otherwise have little to offer. Explorers will appreciate a 15-km (9-mile) detour eastward from the village of Yenişakran to **Köseler**, where an attendant indicates the 2.5-km (1½-mile) route over a stony path and through a river valley to the ruins of the Pergamene colony of ★ **Aigai**. The market hall alone, over 80m (262ft) long and dating from the 3rd or 2nd century BC, is worth the arduous trek. Also worth investigating are the theatre, sections of the town wall and an old cobbled path. South of the oil port of **Aliağa** lie the two Foças (270km/167 miles).

Phokaia, once an important port, was situated near ★ **Eski Foça** (pop. 12,000). Explorers set sail from here in the 7th century BC to found Marseille and Nice. The **Taşkule**, a rough-hewn grave monument 6m (20ft) high some 7km (4 miles) outside the village, is of particular interest as is the **Şeytan Hamamı**, a grave chamber carved out of the rock (in the south). The town itself boasts a **Temple of Athena** and in 1991 a **theatre** was uncovered. The Genoese castle is in poor condition. That the town was once inhabited by Greeks is apparent from the traditional town houses with their elevated portals. There are a number of narrow beaches in the vicinity.

View of bay from the Taşkule

The history of **Yeni Foça** (pop. 1,000) on the north coast of the peninsula does not reach back quite so far, but interesting features include the various stone tower houses in the Italian tradition, which are of Genoese origin.

Yeni Foça beach

Menemen (307km/190 miles; pop. 30,000) just off the motorway into İzmir is noted for its hand-painted pottery. Follow the Gediz river valley to Manisa (*see page 31*), otherwise continue straight to İzmir..

The slow way round İzmir

Route 2

★★ İzmir – the key to the Aegean

With a population of 2.1 million, İzmir, formerly Smyrna, is Turkey's third-largest city but, if zest for life could be measured, then it would almost certainly be top of the list. Whatever the time of day, the city throbs with life. İzmir is a town with colour, atmosphere and style and, to its credit, it can boast many fine restaurants lining the Kordon, its famous promenade, quaint narrow alleys in the bazaar and a busy bay where ferries with their muffled sirens shuttle across to the northern districts of the town. İzmir does have its fair share of environmental problems, however. In addition to the poverty-ridden slums, traffic is chaotic and there is often a smog warning signal in the late afternoon. The bay is biologically dead.

Spices in the bazaar

Islam arrived in AD1100

History

History comes alive in İzmir. The unassuming tea houses where bubble pipes continue to gurgle, the small bookshops where bearded Moslems sell holy texts, the families walking in single file through the old town led by the senior member – all serve as symbols of İzmir's more recent history as a city of Islam. This period began about AD1100 when a Turkish pirate by the name of Çağa – he is honoured by a statue on Konak Square – mounted a display of Asian power in the Aegean. Few buildings remain from the period of Turkish rule, which did not gain a firm foothold until the 15th century. Only one or two warehouses and mosques in the bazaar quarter and the arches of the Ottoman aqueduct in the Kızıl district of the town testify to the lasting importance of this port. Little remains of ancient Smyrna either. The oldest ruined site is found in the outer suburb of Bayraklı (*see page 31*). Aeolian Greeks founded the first city of Smyrna there on Bronze Age foundations in about 1000BC. Around 800BC the city joined the league of Ionian cities and it is said that the blind poet Homer was among the inhabitants of Smyrna at about that time. After the second Greek invasion under Alexander the Great (334BC), the centre of the town was moved to the south, close to the district by the bazaar known now as Namazgâh. All of the ancient monuments, whether they be the foundation walls at Bayraklı or the Roman agora in Namazgâh, have been built over, so traces of Smyrna's wealth can now only be seen in the Archaeological Museum.

Shoeshine time

Smyrna burns

In September 1922 Smyrna was burnt to the ground, almost 30,000 homes were destroyed and the bitter dispute between Greeks and Turks took a high toll in lives. Many of the weaknesses of the Ottoman empire had long been exposed and after World War I all of Asia Minor fell under the guardianship of the major western powers, including their allies the Greeks. However, the occupying forces underestimated the resistance of the Turkish people, who rallied around Atatürk (*see page 15*) to create an army of liberation. They won battle after battle and eventually reached the Aegean coast which had been settled from the 12th century by Greeks. The final confrontation took place in Smyrna. When the Allies fled, they left behind a blazing inferno.

29

The Culture Park was laid out at the point where Smyrna had burnt at its fiercest. Although the 1923 Treaty of Lausanne brought the conflict to an end, the consequences were severe for the Greek population of Asia Minor. A population exchange was agreed and a total of 1.3 million Greeks were expelled from Turkish soil, while some 450,000 Turks in Greece were forced to return to their homeland. The Greek name of Smyrna was abandoned to be replaced by its Turkish equivalent: İzmir.

Sights

The bustling **Konak Square ❶** or **Konak Meydanı** lies at the heart of the town. Situated only a few yards from the sea, it links the ferry port with the inner city and the bazaar. As well as several department stores, the principal sights are the **Konak Mosque** (1754) with its colourful tiles and the ornate Moorish-style Clock Tower which was built at the behest of the sultan in 1901.

The Konak Mosque with tile detail

The★ **bazaar** with its narrow alleys extends eastwards from Konak Square. It is worth seeking out the two caravanserais, **Çakoloğlu Hanı** and **Kızlarağazı Hanı ❷** both of which date from the 18th century, the **Hisar**

mosque **3** of 1597 and the **Şadırvan mosque 4** of 1636. But first-time visitors will be fascinated by the thriving shopping area and lively artisan quarter.

The agora

The ★ **agora 5** (Tuesday to Sunday 9am–noon and 1.30–5.30pm), the old **Roman market place** in the Namazgâh quarter, consists of an open central courtyard surrounded by a two-storey colonnade. The Corinthian columns date from the 2nd century AD but a Hellenistic agora is known to have stood here before then. On the west side 13 columns with fine capitals have survived, while a number of Ottoman gravestones testify to the later use of the square as an Islamic graveyard.

Situated on Mount Pagos (160m/525ft) **Kadifekale 6**, meaning 'Velvet Castle', dates from Byzantine times. The older ramparts and towers that Alexander the Great built were removed a long time ago. The park and tea gardens are popular with families and courting couples and the view over the city is impressive.

Poseidon and Demeter at the Archaeological Museum

The ★ **Ethnological Museum** with its displays of Turkish furniture and traditional crafts and the ★★ **Archaeological Museum 7** (Tuesday to Sunday 9am–5pm) stand on the hillside overlooking Konak Meydanı. Both are well worth a visit – particularly the archaeological museum, which contains many of the finest discoveries from the ancient sites of western Anatolia.

★ **Kordon 8** to the north of Konak Square is famous

30

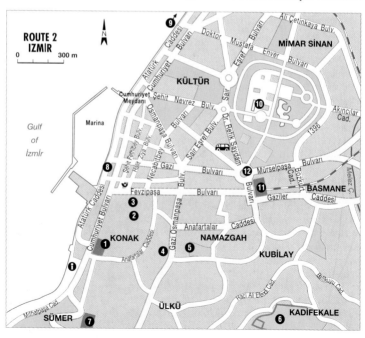

ROUTE 2
IZMIR
0   300 m

for its fish restaurants, cafés and bars. Old-fashioned horse-drawn carts pass up and down this promenade – or Atatürk Caddesi to use its proper name – which in the afternoon is often cooled by a sea breeze. In the evening, when the Kordon is closed to cars, brass lanterns illuminate this lively cosmopolitan boulevard. The **Atatürk Museum**  (daily 9am–noon and 1–5pm) at the north end of the Kordon occupies a house where the republic's founder once lived. On display are some of the celebrated leader's personal possessions.

Trade fair at the Culture Park

The **Culture Park** ❿ offers the residents of İzmir both rest and relaxation away from the unremitting hustle and bustle of the city centre. There are restaurants, a small lake, a swimming pool and tennis courts. Every year it is the site for the *fuar*, an important trade fair.

Many cheap hotels and restaurants can be found in the district around **Basmane Station** ⓫ and **Dokuz Eylül Square** ⓬, while on weekend mornings there are bargains galore at the flea market.

Excursions

31

★ **Bayraklı** (Old Smyrna), a green hill in the stony suburbs of İzmir, lies 8km (5 miles) to the north of the city. House foundations, lines of streets and the polygonal supporting wall of a temple are all that remain of the ancient Greek settlement of Smyrna (*see page 29*). The most interesting finds unearthed by the archaeologists can be seen in Izmir's Archaeological Museum.

★ **Manisa** (29km/18 miles) was known in antiquity as Magnesia. It lies to the northeast of İzmir over a 675-m (2,214-ft) pass. Although little has survived from the town's early past – a few finds are displayed in Manisa's ★ **Archaeological Museum** – many Islamic buildings remain. Of these, the ★ **Ulu Cami** (1376–7) and ★★ **Muradiye Camii** (1583–6) are definitely worth closer inspection. The latter was built by the master architect Sinan, and is without doubt the finest mosque on the entire coast. Near Manisa on a steep incline above the Akpınar waterworks stands a Hittite monument. ★ **Taş Suret** or Stone Picture is how the Turks describe this oversized image of a bearded mountain god.

A local guide

Kemalpaşa (34km/21 miles) lies over the Belkahve pass. The principal sight is **Kız Kalesi**, a ruined palace known as the 'Maiden's Castle'. It was here in 1244 that Konstanze von Hohenstaufen, the daughter of Frederick II, the Holy Roman Emperor, married the Byzantine Emperor John III. The three-storey building with alternating layers of reddish bricks and white stones is about 15m (50ft) high. Visitors to Kemalpaşa ought not to miss the ★ **Eti Baba** (Hittite Father), which can be found east of the road to Torbalı. The 2-m (6-ft) high bas-relief shows

the profile of a ruler carrying a lance, bow and sword. It is thought to depict the young king Targasnalli, who lived in the 13th century BC.

The Çesme peninsula

Leave the modern İzmir to Çeşme motorway near Güzelbahçe and head south through the little market town of Seferhisar and then west towards **Sığacık**, a picturesque port with 15th-century Genoese ramparts and rows of low houses. It is worth stopping off here, if only to enjoy the fresh fish served in the modest restaurants. A road winds up a slope to a wooded summit (and from there down to a fine sandy beach on the right) and past picnic sites beneath pine trees to ★ **Teos**, an ancient Ionian city set in a delightful spot. The poet Anakreon was born here about 580BC. The Greek guild of actors and musicians, or the 'Technites of Dionysos' as the players were known, had their headquarters in the town and, of course, the main **temple** in Teos (3rd century BC) was dedicated to Dionysos. Some of the columns have been rebuilt. Also look out for the small but well-preserved **odeion** (a round building where music and plays were performed) with its 11 or 12 rows of seating and the Roman **theatre** further up the slopes of the acropolis, but only the pit of the auditorium remains. There is, however, a splendid view over the Aegean and the many offshore islands from this commanding position.

Sığacık

Down by the beach, where a few kiosks and bars have opened up to cater for the summer campers and sunbathers, the remains of the ancient **quay** can still be made out.

It is worth making a short detour to the picturesque village of ★ **Ildır**. The Ionian town of **Erythrai** once stood here by the Aleon river and much of interest has survived: sections of the peculiar red and white town wall, a theatre, the foundations of a grand tomb, a Hellenistic and a Roman villa and traces of ancient dwellings. There is also a fine view of the sea from the acropolis.

The beach at Çeşme

★ **Çeşme** (60km/37 miles; pop. 21,000) is a modern and lively resort with fine sandy beaches. It used to be the port for Erythrai (*see above*). During the 14th and 15th centuries the Genoese rulers of Chíos fortified the town with a **castle** which the Ottoman sultan Beyazit later extended. In 1770 a decisive battle in the Russo-Turkish war took place in the straits between Chíos and Çeşme when almost the whole of the Ottoman fleet was wiped out.

The view from the castle

The present name of the town refers to the sulphur springs which flow from the hillsides. The healing properties of the water in an otherwise dry and barren peninsula attracted rheumatism sufferers to the ancient resort of Ilıca nearby.

32

Route 3

Where antiquity comes alive

İzmir to Bodrum and Marmaris via Ephesus (335km/207 miles) *See map on page 34*

Temple of Apollo at Klaros

33

The finest section of the Asia Minor coast begins 75km (46 miles) south of İzmir. A series of outstanding sites of antiquity such as Ephesus, Priene and Miletus are dotted around the plains, while by the coast the towns of Bodrum, Marmaris and Datça have become lively and popular holiday resorts. Visitors venturing into the hinterland will discover amazing white limestone terraces at Pamukkale and ancient Herakleia, set in a romantic spot beneath the wild peaks of the Beşparmak. But despite the holiday hotspots and the crowds besieging the historic sites, there are still places where peace and quiet reign, such as the Samsun Dağı National Park or the Great Maeander delta. There can hardly be anywhere else on the Mediterranean coast which offers so much within such a small area. To make the most of this route, allow at least four days.

Seeing the sights in Selçuk

After the chaotic roads south of İzmir, the coastal village of **Gümüldür** (50km/31 miles) is a peaceful haven, although on summer weekends the beaches here, as in **Özdere**, are very popular with İzmir families. Ancient **Klaros,** where the foundations of a Temple of Apollo lie in marshy terrain, is situated nearby, and at **Notion** it is worth climbing the hill above two pretty beaches to view the city wall, town hall and theatre.

On the way to Selçuk and Ephesus, take a detour to **Birgi**, where one of the oldest mosques on the west coast (1312–13) and a splendid 19th-century residence can be admired.

Souvenirs at Ephesus

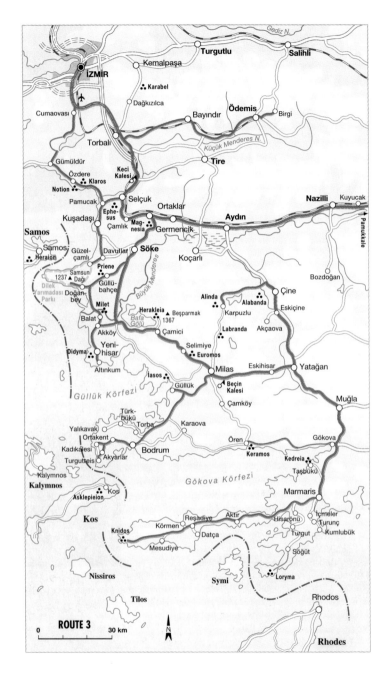

34

ROUTE 3

0 — 30 km

Selçuk/Ephesus

The town of Selçuk (75km/46 miles; pop. 19,000) was formerly ★★★ **Ephesus**, the city which attracted pilgrims to its Temple of Artemis as early as the 6th century BC. Even then, the silting up of the Kaystros (now Küçük Menderes) caused constant problems. The settlement was first moved about 560BC and again at the beginning of the 3rd century BC. At around the time of the birth of Christ, the third Ephesus, the ruined site of today, was an important city in Roman Asia Minor and later also in the Christian world. Mary and the evangelist John are said to have spent their final days here, but in the 3rd century AD, the Goths overran and plundered the city and it was later devastated by malaria. A fourth, Byzantine, Ephesus grew up on the hill where the St John Basilica now stands. Since the conquest of the town by the Seljuks in the 11th century, the town has borne their name, Selçuk.

A ruined Byzantine fortress stands on Ayasoluk hill by Selçuk's main street. The huge **Gate of Persecution** was built with stones from the Roman stadium. It takes its name from the ancient relief which shows the death of the Trojan hero Hector, an event which the Christians interpreted as a martyrdom.

The Gate of Persecution

35

The construction of the **St John Basilica [A]** on the **citadel** was ordered by the Roman emperor Justinian in the 6th century AD above what was thought to be the grave of St John. The vast interior is clad with marble and the whole complex was so big that to accommodate the forecourt – now a terrace with a fine view over the Maeander plain – the hill had to be extended. Beneath the citadel stands the ★ **İsa Bey Mosque [B]**, which was built in 1375, incorporating columns from ancient Ephesus in the courtyard. The entrance, surmounted by a minaret, displays stalactite decorations and an ornamental woven effect created with black and white marble.

St John Basilica: detail

İsa Bey Mosque

Among the attractions in the **Archaeological Museum [C]** (daily 8.30am–5pm) are two statues of the Ephesian Artemis, the Socrates fresco from an Ephesian residence, known as Eros on the Dolphin and sections of a 2nd-century Parthian frieze.

Little remains of the sacred **Artemision [D]**, one of the Seven Wonders of the Ancient World, apart from a few rebuilt columns now used by storks as sites for their nests. The first temple, built in the 6th century BC, went up in flames in 356BC. The fire-raiser Herostratos claimed that by his actions he had ensured a mention in the history books. After Alexander the Great offered a sacrifice in the ruins in 334BC, the townsfolk decided to rebuild the temple. After 120 years, the new Hellenistic Artemision was ready, but built on a stone platform. It stood for another 500 years before the invading Goths destroyed it. It is about

2km (1¼ miles) from the two entrances to the ruined site. Before reaching the ticket office by the lower entrance the early Christian burial ground known as the **Seven Sleepers [E]** can be seen. Seven boys, enclosed in a cave, slept through the Christian persecution during the 3rd century. The 2nd-century AD **Vedius gymnasium [F]**, the **stadium [G]** dating from the Emperor Nero's time and a Byzantine **palace** are all located outside the car park which is well supplied with souvenir stalls and snack bars.

After entering the site (daily 8.30am–4.30pm), instead of making straight for the theatre, turn right to the ruined **Church of the Virgin Mary [H]**. Important Ecumenical Council meetings were held here in AD431 and AD449. To the southwest lies the **harbour gymnasium** (2nd century AD). However crowded Ephesus may be, at least here it is possible to let the magic of the ancient world penetrate the soul.

The theatre area commences with the ★ **Arcadiana [I]**, an 11-m (35-ft) wide colonnaded street which leads down to the harbour. On the left is the ★★ **great theatre [J]**, where once the silversmith Demetrios, who feared the spread of Christianity would ruin his business selling souvenirs to the Artemis pilgrims, stirred up trouble for the apostle Paul. In the 2nd century AD, there was space here for about 25,000 spectators. There is a stunning view from the highest seats, some 30m (100ft) above the orchestra.

The ★★ **Celsus Library [K]** ranks, perhaps, as the finest sight in ancient Ephesus. It has been painstakingly rebuilt by Austrian archaeologists using only the tools that were available to the workmen at the time. Celsus, to whom the library was dedicated, was governor of the Roman province of Asia around AD105. When Celsus died,

Warding off the evil eye

The Celsus Library

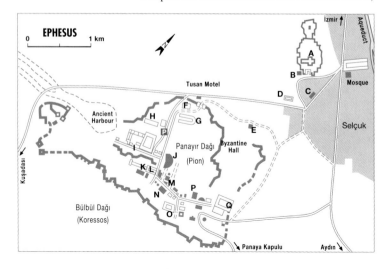

Arch of the Temple of Hadrian

his son honoured his achievements by building this ornate structure which was completed in AD135 and then housed about 12,000 rolled parchments. The qualities that Celsus embodied are depicted in female figures on the facade: from left to right, culture, probity, virtue and wisdom.

On the right stands an equally splendid carved ★ **market gate**, built at around the time of Christ. It leads into the **lower agora [L]**, a large square with 110-m (350-ft) long sides. It was once surrounded by colonnades.

The lower agora

The ★ **Street of Curetes** once formed part of the pilgrim's way, probably the reason why it does not conform to the chequerboard town plan. The local guides like to point out the inconspicuous ruins opposite the library. With its vast number of rooms, it was thought to be the red light district of Ephesus, but this theory is now doubted. However liberal the attitudes of Roman antiquity may have been, it is extremely unlikely that the brothels would have been quite so close to the town centre.

With its richly decorated entablature (showing the foundation legend) the ★★ **Temple of Hadrian [M]** is a jewel. It honours the Roman emperor (AD117–38) whose skilful policies towards the Orient benefited Ephesus.

The ★ **dwellings on the slope [N]** opposite the Temple of Hadrian bear witness to the grand lifestyle of those who lived in the town centre. Here running water was supplied and the floors and walls were lined with marble, frescoes and mosaics.

Niches in the **Fountain of Trajan**, built in AD102, hold 12 statues. A thirteenth statue shows the emperor Trajan in battle defeating the Dacians and the Parthians.

The upper end of the Street of Curetes joins up with the **Gate of Hercules** and the badly damaged **Memmius monument**. An ancient pavement passes the **Pollio nymphaion** (AD93). Pollio was a wealthy citizen who financed an aqueduct for the town.

The Pollio nymphaion

The **Temple of Domitian [O]** lies diagonally opposite Pollio's fountain but the lower sections are all that remain of this monument to the emperor Domitian (AD81–96) which lies on a raised terrace. A collection of inscriptions and plinths can be viewed in the basement.

The **upper agora** (160 x 58m/525 x 190ft), once surrounded on three sides by colonnades, stands at the eastern end of the Street of Curetes opposite the ★ **prytaneion [P]**. This was the town's council chamber where the magistrates assembled and the sacred fire burned, guarded day and night by the Curetes (priests). The two large statues of Artemis (in the museum) originated from here. The adjoining ★ **odeion**, a small theatre for 1,500 spectators, was used for political meetings.

The odeion

Getting ahead

Just past the ruins of the **Varius Baths** lies the monumental **east gymnasium [Q]** followed by the foundation walls of the **Magnesian Gate**, the old entrance to the town (1st century AD).

On the wooded slopes of Ala Dağ (7km/4 miles) stands the ★ **House of the Virgin Mary** (Turkish = *Meryamana*). It is said that Mary, the mother of Jesus, spent her last days here. In Byzantine times the foundation walls of this simple structure were converted into a chapel. The discovery of the house came about following the visions of a German nun by the name of Katharina Emmerich (1774–1824). The Catholic church now maintains a pilgrims' hostel nearby.

In 1970 **Kuşadası** (93km/58 miles; pop. 25,000) was still a quiet fishing village, but since then one hotel after another has been built, not to mention about 150 pensions. Even so the beaches here are modest. (Vast holiday villages adjoin the main sandy beaches in the south.) During the high season and particularly when the cruise ships dock, the lanes and alleys throng with people. Kuşadası was founded around 1340 by the Genoese and was christened Scala Nova (New Harbour), as it was intended as a replacement for the silted up harbour at Ephesus. It is still possible to identify sections of the old town wall and the offshore island of Güvercin Ada (Dove Island) possesses a small Genoese fortress that now serves as a night club. The island became Turkish in the 17th century and Ökuz Mehmetpaşa Han, the Ottoman caravanserai by the harbour, dates from around that time.

Colonnade detail

To the south of Selçuk lies the village of **Çamlık** (84km/52 miles). The 'Sultanköy' carpet centre gives western visitors a very warm welcome. One of the prized exhibits in the railway museum is a locomotive that worked the legendary Baghdad line. About 12km (7 miles) further on is the valley of the Great Maeander (Büyük Menderes).

Maeander Valley and Pamukkale

For the 160-km (99-mile) journey through the Maeander river valley, it is the cultivation of grapes, olives and figs that dominates the landscape. The silt-laden Maeander itself flows sluggishly westward but it is usually too far from the road to be seen clearly. At **Denizli** a road branches off to one of the natural wonders of Turkey: the limestone terraces of ★★ **Pamukkale**.

Denizli farmers

★★ **Pamukkale**, the site of ancient Hierapolis, is famous for its hot spring water (35°C/95°F) which is rich in calcium carbonate and carbon dioxide. The chalk deposits, which have formed bizarrely shaped, dazzling white terraces and domes, make one of the most spectacular natural landscapes in Turkey. However, in recent years the warm water has been tapped by an increasing number of hotel swimming pools in the village below. The shortage of water and the shoes of countless tourists have discoloured the terraces and setting foot on them is now restricted.

Frontinus Gate at Hierapolis

Sightseers are often so overwhelmed by the white rocks that they forget the ruins at **Hierapolis**. But try not to miss the baths (including a museum) and the theatre. From here stroll down the colonnaded street through the Byzantine city gate to the Frontinus Gate, behind which lies ★ **north necropolis**, the biggest city of the dead in the whole of Asia Minor.

Other interesting ancient sites exist in the Maeander valley and in order to appreciate them to the full, stay overnight in one of the thermal bath hotels on the Hierapolis plateau (eg Tusan, Koru, Mistur, Pamukkale). **Aphrodisias** is famous for its statuary and stadium, probably the best example in antiquity, **Laodiceia** for its two theatres and a stadium and **Nyssa** for its theatre and council chamber for elders.

Paddling at Pamukkale

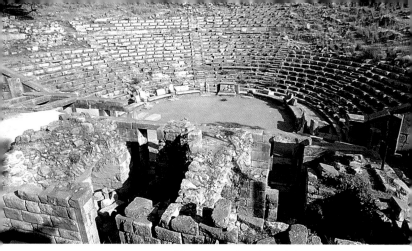

The theatre at Priene

The coast road southwards from Selçuk to Bodrum passes **Magnesia on the Maeander** (98km/60 miles). This ancient town possesses a Byzantine **town wall** and the huge remains of some Roman **barracks**. Capitals and the foundation walls remain from one of Asia Minor's most important Ionic temples, the **Temple of Artemis** (end of 3rd century BC). **Söke** (118km/73 miles; pop. 52,000) serves as a busy trading centre for the villages of the lower Maeander valley. Market day is Wednesday and the best day to see the town come alive.

Cotton harvest time

★★ **Priene** (137km/84 miles), one of the oldest Ionian towns, is situated above the pretty village of **Güllübahçe**. The first Priene was a port at the foot of the mountain where the waters of the Latmian Gulf once lapped, but this land is now occupied by the meadows of the Maeander plain. From the ruins of the town, which was founded about 350BC, it is possible to detect the work of the town-planner Hippodamus, as the streets are laid out in a chequerboard pattern. There is a road to the ruins (daily 8.30am–6.30pm) from the village square.

The 3rd-century BC ★★ **theatre** originally had 50 rows of seats which clung to the hillside in the traditional Greek style. A long stage building closes off the auditorium to the south and a Byzantine church stands alongside.

Temple of Athena

The ★★ **Temple of Athena**, whose pillars are visible from afar against the rocks of the acropolis, was dedicated to Priene's patron saint. It was built between 350 and 330BC with financial assistance from Alexander the Great. Even during the Roman empire this structure, with its grand columns, was regarded as a classic of the Ionic order. Some splendid **stone seats** for the archons can be seen in the orchestra and an ornate **altar** stands outside the temple, while to the west lies the residential quarter of Priene.

Follow a steep road, flanked by the 116-m (380-ft) **sacred stoa** (2nd century BC), down to the state **agora**. This was where the town's politics were enacted. At its perimeter stood a Temple of Zeus (a castle has since been built over it), the ★ **bouleuterion** and the **prytaneion**, where the magistrate lived.

Bouleuterion remains

The most beautiful part of the Maeander delta with its marshy lagoons, bird habitats (lesser kestrels and flamingo colonies) and abundant fishing grounds is inaccessible by car. It is possible to explore the area on foot either from Akköy or the tiny village of Doğanbey to the west of Priene, although for an all-embracing view of the delta out as far as the island of Samos, climb the hillsides of Samsun Dağı (1,237m/4,057ft). Start out from Güzelçamlı on the north side (about 2 hours; guide recommended).

★★ **Miletus** lies about 17km (10 miles) from Güllübahce/Priene. Old Miletus, 'Queen of the Aegean', once dominated the waters of the gulf from a promontory, but sediment from the river has blocked the bay and now the ruins of the city lie just above sea level.

Baths at Miletus

Miletus was the political and cultural centre of eastern Greece. This Ionian city acquired its wealth from the export of expensive purple robes, and founded several colonies, many on the Black Sea. In the 6th century BC the philosophers Thales, Anaximander and Anaximenes brought fame to Miletus and, later on, the architect and town planner Hippodamus applied his chequerboard layout when he rebuilt the city following its destruction by the Persians in 494BC. After St Paul brought Christianity in AD51, Miletus was ruled by the emirs of Milas in Balat, as the nearby village is known (named after the Byzantine castle of Palatia).

The ★★ **theatre** offers the best overview of the ruined site. Built in the 2nd century AD, it offered seating for 15,000 spectators. During the 8th century, the Byzantines built a castle on the hill as protection against marauding Arab pirates.

The theatre

The ★ **Baths of Faustina** date from the 2nd century AD and the name derives from the wife of the Roman emperor Marcus Aurelius. This sumptuous complex includes changing rooms, frigidarium, caldarium and sauna. A lion sculpture and a figure of the river god Maeander in the marble frigidarium are indications of the prosperity that Miletus once enjoyed.

The north **agora** or market place measured 90 x 43m (295 x 141ft) and was surrounded by a colonnade. The Doric **stoa**, part of which has been rebuilt, gives some idea of the grandeur of the town's business quarters. Other Roman ruins can be seen around the huge agora and to the north lie **Lion Bay** and the remains of the **harbour monument** with its decorative relief. The south agora, measuring 196 x 164m (642 x 537ft) was the biggest market place in antiquity. The bouleuterion could accommodate 1,200 citizens on 18 rows of seating.

İlyas Bey Camii stands between the south agora and the modern museum. It is one of the few interesting mosques on the west coast. İlyas Bey, an emir of the Menteşe dynasty from Milas (*see page 43*), commissioned the mosque in 1404. It was constructed almost entirely of marble from the ruins of Miletus. The splendid sculpture in the interior is typical of the Seljuk era.

Pottery, grave stelae and robed figures and entablatures are displayed in the **Archaeological Museum**.

Peppers at Didyma

The head of Medusa

42

★★ **Didyma**, or Didim as the Turks call it (167km/103 miles), was once the main temple site for Miletus. In pre-Ionian times the early Anatolians regarded the spring here as a source of sacred water. The ★ **Temple of Apollo** was built in the 6th century BC; its splendour compared favourably with the Temple of Artemis in Ephesus and it became almost as famous as Delphi.

The original temple was destroyed, so in the first half of the 4th century BC Miletus started work on a new *dydimaion* and wealthy benefactors were sought. Seleucids and Ptolemaeans donated money and gold, later the Roman emperors Caligula and Hadrian made contributions but there was still insufficient money to complete the shrine. Work continued for hundreds of years. The last 'heathen emperor', Julian Apostata (AD361–363), wanted to complete it as an anti-Christian symbol but by then there was little support for such grandiose schemes. The temple was finally destroyed by an earthquake in the 15th century.

It nevertheless ranked as one of the most extravagant temples in Turkey and reached almost Egyptian proportions. The 5-m (16-ft) high platform measured 51 x 109m (167 x 357ft) with double rows of 21 pillars on the long sides, 10 on the short sides, plus 12 columns in the forecourt. Each column was 2m (6ft) in diameter and 20m (65ft) high. A flight of steps on the east side leads up to the forecourt with a 14-m (45-ft) high window from where the words of wisdom imparted by the goddess were passed on to the waiting pilgrims. Only the priestesses were allowed to enter the oracle chamber. Here stood a small 11-m (35-ft) high 'mini-temple' with four Ionic pillars where the cult statue of Apollo was placed. The rebuilt pillars, the portal and a head of Medusa still manage to create a mysterious atmosphere among the ruins.

Further south, **Bafa Gölü** appears. This inland lake was once part of the Latmian Gulf where Ionians and Persians

Lake Bafa

met in a naval battle in 496BC. In the 4th century AD deposits from the Great Maeander cut off the gulf from the Aegean. Olive trees are almost as abundant by Lake Bafa as near Edremit. Restaurants and camp-sites line the shores of the lake which is renowned for the quality of its fish.

An uneven track which starts near the village of Çamici leads round the south end of the lake below the Beşparmak (Turkish = five fingers) mountain. In ancient times the 1,357-m (4,450-ft) peak was known as Mount Latmos (louse mountain) and the town at its foot, Herakleia.

The old Carian town of ★★ **Herakleia under Latmos** (151km/93 miles) sits between lake and mountain. The surrounding landscape, the Turkish village architecture (the ruins lie scattered in the village of Kapıkırı) and its sheer size make it an impressive sight. There is plenty to see: the **Temple of Athena**, the **Shrine of Endymion**, the **market place**, the **town hall**, the **theatre**, the imposing **town walls** with towers and a Byzantine **castle** which adds a different dimension.

Herakleia under Latmos
Rock tombs at Herakleia

★ **Euromos** boasts an extraordinarily well-preserved **Temple of Zeus**. Built in the 2nd century AD in Corinthian style, it is certainly worth the short detour. Other remains include the town wall, a theatre, agora and a number of tombs.

43

Milas (179km/110 miles; pop. 30,000) is an attractive little town with a genuine Turkish feel. Look out for the narrow alleys in the bazaar and the Ottoman town houses with bay windows. The town is at its best on Tuesday, when the market is in full swing.

Spices at Milas market

Milas, or Mylasa as it was formerly known, was the original home of the Mausolos family, which later took up residence in Halikarnassos (Bodrum). At the western end of the town, among other ancient remains, eg a Roman town gate and one surviving temple column, lies a Roman **mausoleum**, which is a miniature replica of the famous mausoleum in Bodrum: twelve Corinthian columns on a platform support a pyramid-shaped roof. The Turks call the structure Gümüşkesen (Silver Casket) and it makes a particularly attractive sight in the evening sun.

Milas also possesses two mosques, both of which are certainly worth a visit: **Firuz Bey Camii** (1394) and the restored **Ulu Cami** (1378). Some more buildings which date from the Islamic period can be seen on the ★ **Becin Kalesi** about 5km (3 miles) south of Milas. This plateau was the home of the Menteşe dynasty between the demise of the Seljuks and the emergence of the Ottomans, ie between 1280 and 1426. The dynasty also built the two mosques in the town.

A sacred way linked Carian Mylasa with the isolated **Shrine of Zeus Labrayandos** at ★ **Labranda** (192km/

Labranda

The Temple of Zeus

119 miles) in the heart of an extensive pine forest. From about the 8th century BC, Caria's male elite gathered there, not as one might assume to praise the Greek god Zeus, but his Carian predecessor. His symbol was the double axe. The journey up to Labranda, at an altitude of about 500m (1,650ft), was no less arduous in ancient times than it is now. In summer the track is covered, sometimes knee-deep, in a whitish dust so that taxi drivers from Milas are usually unhappy about making the trip. A four-wheel drive vehicle is really necessary.

The main structures at Labranda date from the 4th century BC when Mausolos and his brother Idrieus ruled Mylasa. They built three sacred meeting places, the **Temple of Zeus Labrayandos** in the Ionic order, a **fountain house** and a **propylaeum** with a 12-m (40-ft) wide staircase. **Baths** were built in Roman times and a Christian **basilica** was added during the Byzantine era.

The peaceful village of **Gülluk** boasts a fine sandy beach and it makes a more restful alternative to Bodrum. At the narrowest point on the peninsula, a road branches off to the new resorts of **Torba** and **Türkbükü** (which have several hotels and holiday villages).

Bodrum

Negotiate the final mountain pass and one of the finest panoramas on the Turkish Mediterranean coast opens up. White houses stacked up against the hillside of ★★ **Bodrum** (230km/142 miles; pop. 20,000) overlook the broad blue bay dominated by the Crusader castle of St Peter.

Bodrum's castle and marina

Ancient Halikarnassos enjoyed its greatest prosperity when the Carian prince Mausolos (377–353BC), who moved his residence here from Mylasa, reigned over almost the whole of the southwest coast of Asia Minor. The monumental tomb in which the ruler finally came to rest was one of the Wonders of the Ancient World and the word 'mausoleum' is derived from Mausolos himself. After the Roman era Halikarnassos faded into obscurity until the Knights of St John established a military base here as a defence against Ottoman troops; however, in 1532, the castle of St Peter finally fell to the Turks. Petronion, as it was known in the Orient, adopted its Turkish name, Bodrum.

Bodrum's rise as tourist citadel began in the 1950s. In high summer nowadays as many as 100,000 holidaymakers throng the narrow alleys, thousands of boats lie at anchor in the marina and life is lived to the full in the bars and discos, often until the early hours. Bodrum itself has little in the way of beaches, so **Gümbet**, the nearest bay to the west, is the main draw for beach enthusiasts. Windsurfing, diving and waterskiing are just some of the activities available. The next bay along at **Bitez** offers even more, but for a gentler pace try **Yalıkavak** (sponge-diving centre), **Turgutreis** (miles of sandy beaches), **Kadıkalesi**, **Gündoğan**, **Gölköy** or **Akyarlar** (an old Greek village). For quite how long these resorts can offer a quieter life is not clear: an unstoppable onslaught by hotel developers has seen one hotel village after another appear along this stretch of coast. Despite the advance of tourism, away from the coast there is still plenty to enjoy: old bridle paths lead into the interior and ancient ruins, shepherds' camps and domed cisterns await exploration.

Sponges for sale

Sadly, little remains of the world-famous **mausoleion** (daily except Wednesday 8am–noon and 1–5pm) apart from the foundation walls. The Knights of St John dismantled the 40-m (130-ft) high tomb and used the stones to build St Peter's castle. A model in the museum gives some indication of what the mausoleum looked like. The ancient Greek-style **theatre** (probably 3rd century BC) lies on the hillside above the town. It is separated into two tiers with accommodation for about 12,000 spectators and offers a spectacular view over Bodrum and the castle, particularly in the late afternoon.

The theatre above the town

The ★ **Castle of St Peter** has become a symbol for Bodrum. This medieval fortress is also a museum (Tuesday to Sunday 8.30am–noon and 3–7pm). The Knights of St John started work on the huge complex in 1402 and the project lasted for more than a hundred years. When Sultan Suleyman captured the Crusaders' headquarters on Rhodes, many of their outposts also fell into Turkish hands. The recommended route for visitors to follow in the museum is well signposted. Exhibits include Mycenean pottery (15th–12th century BC), the only frieze panels from the mausoleum (4th century BC) that remained in Bodrum, discoveries made by underwater archaeologists in the

Some local colour

waters off Bodrum and artefacts from the Middle Ages. Of particular interest are the contents of a Carian princess's tomb. A likeness of the princess has been reconstructed by an English forensic specialist.

Stratonikeia

The main route from Milas (*see page 43*) to Muğla passes through isolated pine forests. Ancient ★ **Stratonikeia** lies near the abandoned Turkish village of **Eskihisar** in the middle of a brown coal mining area. The ruins here include a fine theatre, an Ionic temple and a gymnasium.

Near **Yatağan** (224km/138 miles; pop. 12,000) the main road heads north through the bizarre Çine Çayı valley towards Aydın. Beyond Çine close to Araphisar lie the ruins of **Alabanda**. Perhaps of more interest, however, would be a visit to the Carian town of ★ **Alinda**, which occupies an impressive spot across the fields beside the village of Karpuzlu.

Alabanda

As well as the town walls, a theatre, a 100-m (325-ft) long market hall and numerous graves have survived.

Muğla (251km/155 miles) is situated to the southeast of Yatağan. This provincial capital, set on the edge of the İkizce Dağı, is an attractive town with a lively bazaar. The main road south descends by about 700m (2,000ft) presenting motorists with a splendid view of the Gulf of Gökova. A new road leads to **Keramos**, an old Carian town with some temple foundations and sarcophagi. The site is close to the village of Ören, which can offer a sandy beach and modest private accommodation.

The Marmaris road, first shaded by a marvellous avenue of eucalyptus trees, then winds through dense pine forests. In **Taşbükü** (just under 6km/4 miles), it is possible to hire a boat to nearby **Sedir Adası** (Cedar Island) notable for the ruins of ancient Kedreia and for a 20-m (65-ft) wide beach of very fine sand.

Marmaris

Harbouring dreams

Once an idyllic fishing port, set in a near-perfect natural harbour, ★ **Marmaris** (310km/192 miles) is now perhaps the most popular of all the resorts on the entire Turkish coast. At first sight, the broad, picturesque bay seems to promise much, but with the onset of mass tourism – mainly in the eastern suburb of İcmeler – the place has certainly lost some of its appeal. It is popular with Turkish celebrities and the smart set, particularly in May for the International Yacht Festival and in June for the Music and Entertainment Festival. But these are the consequences: crowds of people in the narrow streets, daylight robbery in the restaurants by the harbour and extortionate prices in the bazaar.

On the other hand, Marmaris can provide all the facilities that tourists could wish for. Windsurfing, diving and sailing are all within easy reach and the new marina is one of the biggest in the Aegean.

The prettiest area of Marmaris is the old town around the Ottoman **Marmara Kalesi**, a castle built by Suleyman the Magnificent. Rather than struggle through the busy bazaar, take a peaceful stroll along the narrow alleys lined by Greek houses.

High season on the beach

Just beyond Marmaris, the Turkish west coast ends in two long peninsulas which on the map look like a lobster's pincers. On the southern **Bozburun peninsula** tourism is still in its infancy, but villages such as **Bozburun** and **Sögüt** offer basic accommodation and restaurants. Well worth seeking out, although it is only accessible by boat, is the ★ **Bozukkale** (destroyed castle) situated at the extreme tip of the peninsula. It was built in the 2nd century BC and belonged to the town of Loryma. The whole of the wall, including tower reinforcements and five gates, have survived intact. And after a tour of the ancient site, the beach is close at hand.

The **Reşadiye peninsula** extends westwards for over 100km (60 miles) to within only a few miles of the Greek island of Kos. The fishing village of **Datça** (78km/48 miles from Marmaris) has become a popular tourist destination and one that is certainly quieter than Marmaris. But if that is not peaceful enough, then try a boat trip to one of the isolated sandy bays.

Datça is more peaceful

47

On the extreme tip of the Reşadiye peninsula lie the ruins of ancient ★ **Knidos** (35km/22 miles from Datça, uneven track). In the 7th century BC it was the centre of the Doric league of city-states and the site for a Sanctuary of Apollo, although Aphrodite, the patron saint of mariners, was the main deity for Knidos as the town lived from the sea. Two harbours, a military one and a commercial one (where the pleasure boats now anchor), testify to the town's illustrious past.

Knidos

The oldest dwellings from ancient Knidos are found on the offshore peninsula – originally an island – while the major public buildings remain on the mainland. These include a **theatre** (in a poor sate of repair), an **odeion** for about 4,500 spectators and what is thought to be the **Temple of Apollo**, a round structure supported by columns in which the famous statue by Praxiteles once stood. A well-preserved sundial from the Roman period can be seen near the Corinthian **temple** while the Sanctuary of Apollo was probably located on the terrace above the small theatre. The strong walls with towers and gates on the **acropolis** are an impressive sight. Between the two ancient harbours, restaurants offer fresh fish, but there is no accommodation available.

Route 4

Beaches, fishing villages and rock tombs

Marmaris to Antalya via Kaş (420km/260 miles)

This route follows the Lycian coast, which is famous for its extraordinary rock tombs, and passes through Fethiye where the delightful beach at Ölü Deniz beckons. Against the backdrop of the huge Beydagları mountains lie long sandy beaches and bays enclosed by rocky headlands. Ruined sites in the Taurus woods await exploration. Even here, many of the villages still reveal their Greek past. Between the mountains, fertile plains are intensively farmed. To take in all the sights, a good three days will be necessary. Fethiye, Kaş and the lively town of Kemer can all offer accommodation.

Köyceğiz (62km/38 miles) lies to the east of Marmaris (*see pages 46–7*). It is a small village on the northern shores of Lake Köyceğiz. Tourism is still at an early stage here and there are no beaches. The village's appeal centres around the smooth lakeside waters – the lake was once a deep seawater bay that has since silted up.

The fishermen in the south of the lake offer boat trips from Dalyan to ancient **Kaunos**, Iztuzu beach and the mud springs at Sultaniye. The **rock tombs**, visible from the har-

Lycian rock tombs

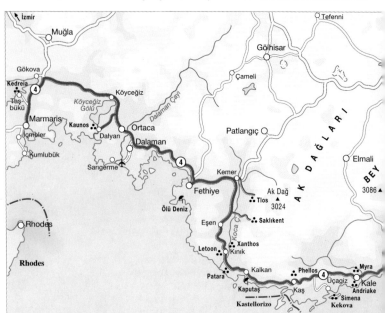

bour on the east bank, date from the 4th century BC and have facades like temples. Extending as far as Kale (Myra), they give an insight into Lycian civilisation. The decline of Kaunos coincided with the silting up of the harbour, but a **theatre**, which offers a fine view over the coast, a Byzantine fortress and temple foundations near the harbour, now 2km (1¼ miles) from the sea, have survived.

Leave Köyceğiz and continue through Ortaca and the **Dalaman** plain with its airport and Sarıgerme's long sandy beach (modern luxury hotels). Ahead lies **Fethiye** (130km/ 80 miles; pop. 38,000), a little town with a sheltered harbour set in a deep, idyllic gulf that once played an important historic role. Originally known as Telmessos, it was the first Lycian town to make contact with the ancient Greeks. During the Ottoman years, under the name of Meğri, it became the principal port for southwestern Asia Minor. No wonder that once the Greeks had been expelled by Atatürk, the town was renamed Fethiye (Victory). An earthquake in 1957 destroyed many of the older buildings in the town. Nevertheless, Fethiye remains an attractive spot and has become a thriving tourist centre in recent years. Alongside numerous pubs, discotheques and bars, the downtown area is lined with countless gift shops. The restaurants by the quay and the marina are lively during the evenings. During the daytime boats depart from the quayside for the 12 islands in the gulf

Fethiye's waterfront

Gifts to take home

49

ROUTES 4–6

0   30 km

The Lycian **keel sarcophagi** hiding between the houses and the Lycian **rock tombs** on the hillsides above the town create a unique atmosphere. Just how the Lycians imagined life after death is not clear. In fact, very little is known about this tribe that lived in the wild Taurus mountains. They did feature in Homer's epic about the Trojan war (they fought on the side of the Trojans), but they have left very little written evidence behind. It is certain, however, that they must have had some unusual ideas about death. Although several stages of development have been identified, there is one thing in common: the dead were not left to rest in the earth, but always high up in rock chambers on the acropolis hill or in pillar tombs. The Lycians believed that the souls of the dead would be transported to heaven by harpies – bird-like demons similar to those shown on the pillar tomb in Xanthos.

The tomb of Amyntas

When the Lycian kingdom was culturally in decline during the 4th century BC – having by now come under Greek influence – their Hellenistic temple architecture changed into tomb architecture. Although still in an elevated position above the town, the tombs acquired temple-like facades, copies of the facades of Ionic temples. The ★ **tomb of Amyntas** here in Fethiye is one of the best examples of this type and is well worth a look. There are one or two unfinished tombs in this necropolis and it is possible to work out how they were built. First the gable was carved out, then the stonemasons worked down to the base – in precisely the reverse order a temple would be built.

Ölü Deniz

Try to include an excursion to the ★ **Ölü Deniz** lagoon about 20km (12 miles) to the south of Fethiye. This beautiful headland, where the blue water contrasts with the green pine trees and the white sand, typifies the charm of the Lycian coastline. A charge is now payable to gain

access to the beach/park and there is an abundance of pensions, camp-sites and medium-category hotels close at hand. Just before the descent to Ölü Deniz, a road forks off to the ghost town of **Kaya Köy**, which was abandoned by the Greeks in 1923.

Testing the water

The journey eastwards from Fethiye offers a fine view of the pale peak of **Ak Dağ** (White Mountain; 3,024m/ 9,918ft). Soon the main road (Highway 350) to Antalya branches off to the east, but stay on Highway 400 which follows the coast.

In the **Saklıkent** (Hidden Town) valley, a wild mountain stream breaks through a narrow gorge which – albeit a little shorter – is similar to the famous Samaria gorge on Crete. An unsteady bridge made from planks leads into the valley, where – in a romantic spot above the stream – a restaurant serves Turkish fare. Swimming is permitted, but a few minutes in the ice-cold water will probably be enough.

The ancient town of **Tlos** (177km/110 miles) lies above the road just before Saklıkent. The ruins, including a huge **theatre** and **baths**, surround the tiny village of Kaleköy. The former **acropolis** which was converted into a castle by the Ottomans is visible from a tea house beneath a giant plane tree. Tlos also has a number of **sarcophagi** from early antiquity and some interesting **rock tombs**.

51

Lycian shrine and theatre at Letoon

Situated near the hamlet of Kumluova and at the end of a pleasant tour through the scenic Eşen valley is ★ **Letoon** (205km/127 miles), the most important Lycian shrine. Behind the small **theatre**, which is visible from afar, lie the sculpted sections of a Hellenistic stoa (colonnade). The column stumps now stand in water, offering frogs a good vantage point. The most important relics here are the three **temples** to Leto, Artemis and Apollo, which are sited higher up and consequently have remained dry. Leto was a primitive mother-god, who according to the Greeks bore the children of Zeus. While Apollo was one of the most important Greek gods, Leto was worshipped in Asia Minor. The larger Leto temple dates from the 2nd century BC, but this site was probably considered sacred at the beginning of the 1st millennium BC.

Behind the temples – only the substructure and a few column drums remain – are the ruins of a Roman **nymphaion**, and this too lies underwater. The terrapins attract a lot of attention too. They disappear rapidly into the water at the slightest noise.

Locals at Xanthos

Just a mile or two further east the village of Kınık rests in the shadow of the acropolis at ★ **Xanthos**. Xanthos was the most important city in Lycia from the 7th century BC. It was also probably the seat of its king. When the Persians conquered the city in 545BC, the Lycians, recognising their hopeless position, set their own houses on fire and gave themselves up for slaughter. A similar débâcle occurred in the town during the Roman civil war when Brutus, one of Caesar's killers, demanded money for his decisive battle against Mark Anthony.

The tour begins near the theatre car park, but visitors will already have passed the original location of the Nereid monument, which suffered a fate similar to that of the Pergamon Altar. The English explorer Sir Charles Fellows discovered the temple in 1838 and sent the whole edifice back to London, where it is on display in the British Museum, together with the reliefs. Behind the **theatre** which was hollowed out of the hill stands the most famous relic of Lycian Xanthos, the **Harpy pillar tomb,** and another **tomb** that must have been made up from older tombs probably in the 3rd century BC. The Lycian **acropolis** lies behind the theatre, but the walls at the summit were originally part of a Byzantine **monastery**. Located in front of the theatre the **agora** has an interesting inscribed pillar. The inscription, in the language of the Lycians, tells of a Lycian prince and his deeds in the Peloponnese War. Take a stroll up the hill to the northeast where many typical Lycian tombs are found. There is a delightful view from these idyllic hillsides.

The Harpy pillar tomb

Monastery ruins

The next stop is **Patara** (219km/135 miles; pop. 300), formerly the main port for the Lycians and later the home of a Roman garrison. Patara's most famous son is St Nicholas, who was born here in AD280. The town's demise was precipitated by the same sand which now makes it so popular. Seemingly endless sand dunes have been blown across in front of the harbour and covered the streets. Now one or two buildings protrude from the sand, including the **theatre** on the hillside which provides a commanding view over the whole area. So far only parts of the **necropolis** and one **street** near the Modestus gate have been excavated. A charge is made for access to the site and the beach, but there is also a 4-km (2½-mile) stretch of quiet, sandy beach ahead. A small holiday village has been built a short distance inland.

How the old Greek fishing port of **Kalkan** (225km/139 miles; pop. 1,000) has changed! With its new marina, new hotels and even a new, peaceful, village square, it is a gem of a place and perhaps one to keep quiet about. The village can offer souvenir shops, good restaurants and an amazingly cosmopolitan clientele. Many of the historic sights in the vicinity and the small, but popular **Kaputaş beach** can all be reached by *dolmuş*.

Carpets in Kaş

Like Kalkan, ★ **Kaş** (252km/156 miles) was a small harbour for Greek fishermen, but that is where the similarity ends as the latter has much more to offer. There is

an ancient **theatre** and a Lycian **sarcophagus**, both relics from Lycian Vehinda, whose town centre lay higher up on the steep, barren mountain. A market is held every day on the main square, close to the town's entertainment quarter where hardly anyone goes home before midnight. A fleet of pleasure boats moors in the harbour and many of them offer trips to the village of Üçağız, near ancient Simena, and also the medieval Crusader castle. The Greek island of Kastellórizo (Turkish = Meis Adası) can also be visited. Teimiussa near Üçağız (accessible by road or by boat) is also worth a visit, not just for its ancient tombs but also for the fine fish restaurants.

★ **Myra** (Kale), where St Nicholas was once bishop, is situated 31km (19 miles) to the east on a small plain that is now almost completely hidden by greenhouses. In the heart of the village stands a 6th-century pilgrims' **Church of St Nicholas**. The Normans took the remains of the 4th-century saint to Bari in Italy for safekeeping. The tomb through which oil was poured and then sold for its miraculous powers has also disappeared. The huge Lycian ★ **necropolis** in the north and the Roman **theatre** are all that have survived from ancient Myra.

Andriake used to be the harbour for Myra. The ruins are sparse, but the beach is long and rarely crowded. The little coastal town of **Finike**, further east, has a small harbour and a number of fish restaurants. Like Andriake, it may be worth a brief stop before pressing on to **Limyra** near the village of Zengerler. In Lycian times, it was the seat of the powerful Prince Pericles. On the steep hillsides above the Roman **theatre** stand so-called **keel sarcophagi**, while further up, the temple tomb of Pericles surveys the plain. Byzantine walls indicate the extent of the ancient town. Archaeologists have uncovered the **temple tomb** of Gaius Caesar, the grandson and designated successor to Caesar Augustus.

St Nicholas: relief detail

53

A good choice of fish restaurants

Church of St Nicholas in Myra

Continue eastwards to Antalya via **Kumluca** (303km/ 187 miles) and then up into the **Olimpos National Park** which is dominated by the rugged Beydağları mountains (2,550m/8,364ft). This was where Zeus lived, or so the Greeks believed. An ancient coastal town was known as Olympos, but it is now **Çiralı** (330km/204 miles). Little has survived from the time when it was a lair for Cilician pirates and later, in the Middle Ages, when the Genoese (not unlike the pirates) ran a trading centre here.

Eternal flame at Yanartaş

A curiosity at **Yanartaş** attracts many visitors: a jet of ignited methane gas which was thought, in antiquity, to come from the mouth of a fire-breathing chimera.

Pine trees rustling in the breeze over an ancient cobbled street and three sheltered bays washed by gentle waves – the idyllic but isolated town of **Phaselis** (356km/220 miles) has changed little since it was abandoned during the Arab incursions. The naval harbour behind the **aqueduct** is now a popular beach. Take a stroll from here along the former main road across the peninsula to the commercial harbour, passing the **theatre**, **baths** and **agoras**. In AD114 the emperor Hadrian came ashore near where the pleasure boats now moor and the grand **gate** at the end of the street is dedicated to him.

54

Kemer has been transformed

Kemer (369km/228 miles; pop. 10,500) contrasts sharply with the rural beauty of Phaselis. This once quiet fishing village has been transformed into one of the most popular resorts on the south coast. It is certainly a lively town with a modern look, thanks to the large, new marina and a picturesque park that runs alongside the pebble beach in the north. Kemer is used as a shopping centre for holidaymakers staying at the Çamyuva and Beldibi holiday clubs. Souvenir shops abound, but there are few good restaurants.

Visiting yachts

Antalya (*see page 55*) is now 50km (31 miles) away.

Route 5

★★ Antalya – the 'finest town on the Turkish coast'

Atatürk once described Antalya as the 'finest town on the Turkish coast', but it is now not so easy to share his views. The rapidly growing provincial capital with a population of 400,000 is hidden behind a broadening belt of ugly concrete blocks. It is, however, worth looking beyond this barrier as the town possesses an attractive marina, an old town with some grand Roman and Seljuk buildings, plus some luxuriant Mediterranean vegetation with oleander bushes and spreading palms.

Relaxing with a hookah

History

Antalya, Adalia, Attaleia – three eras linked by one king. The town was founded in the middle of the 2nd century BC by Attalos II, the art-loving king of Pergamon. Not only did he give the town its name, he also fortified the natural harbour. Attaleia, capital of the province of Pamphylia, together with the Pergamene empire, fell to the Romans in 133BC. The apostle Paul came here on his first journey and the Roman emperor Hadrian also visited the town on his way to Egypt in 130BC. Under the Byzantines a defensive wall was built around Adalia, as it was now called. The Crusaders used the town as a base on their journey to the Holy Land during the 12th century, but it was later occupied by the Seljuks. In 1391 the Ottomans conquered Adalia, a town which the 14th-century Arab traveller Ibn Battuta described as 'one of the most splendid cities in the world'. However, the Mongol hordes who occupied the town from 1402 brought catastrophe. It was the 1620s before the Ottomans were able to regain a foothold here.

History is ever present in Antalya

Under Turkish rule, the town became an insignificant provincial centre, but that did not stop the Italians from occupying it at the end of World War I. Kemal Atatürk's war of independence quickly brought any Italian ambitions to an end. In the first years of the Turkish republic, like many other Greek towns, it received a new name. With the opening of the new port and the establishment of a free trade zone, since the mid-1970s Antalya has seen a huge boost in its fortunes. The population has increased tenfold and the old town has undergone a facelift which today's visitors can appreciate.

Sights

Nearly all of Antalya's historic sights are situated in the old town which is ringed by a **wall**. It was last renewed by the Ottomans. Two main thoroughfares, Cumhuriyet Caddesi (with its smart boutiques) and Atatürk Caddesi,

Today's prosperity

Yivli Minare

run alongside the wall. A tour of the old town begins by the **clock tower ❶**, which was once incorporated into the main gate. ★ **Yivli Minare ❷**, or the 'fluted minaret', is an impressive brick structure that soars above the rooftops against a backdrop of the Taurus mountains. The 38-m (125-ft) tower with a shaft that consists of eight half columns was built by the Seljuk sultan Alaeddin Keykobad I (1219–36) probably to commemorate the Seljuk conquest of Antalya. At its base lie the **Eski Cami** mosque, which the Turkman emir Mehmet Bey Hamadoğuları commissioned in 1373 on the site of a Byzantine church, and also the ruins of a Seljuk Koran school. Behind the mosque are two **tombs**: the smaller one for the remains of the wife of the Ottoman sultan Beyazıd II and the larger one for Mehmet Bey. The latter's tomb is still revered as a holy site by the local people. **Mevlevihane**, the monastery of the Whirling Dervishes, is also situated here. It is now used as an art gallery for contemporary artists.

Souvenir stalls and the inevitable touts line the walk down to the ★ **harbour ❸** which lies at the foot of a 50-m (165-ft) high bank. The **Karatay Medrese** with its monumental portal, situated in a side street, dates from the Seljuk era (13th century), while behind the remains of the old harbour entrance lies a small but pleasant entertainment quarter. Its bars, restaurants and discos overlook the quayside from where many of the boat trips depart.

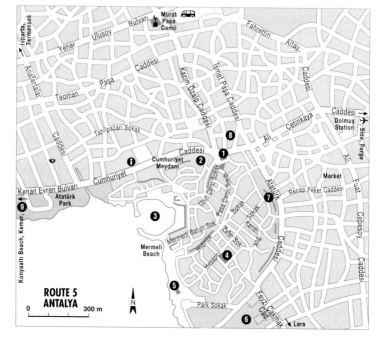

ROUTE 5
ANTALYA
0   300 m

Make the climb up to the old town from the small Mermerli beach at the southern end of the harbour. **Kesik Minare** , the 'stunted minaret' was built at the request of the Ottoman prince Korkut Bey who also converted the older Byzantine church into a mosque. An earthquake destroyed the mosque and its finely sculpted friezes. The upper part of the minaret also fell victim to the earthquake, hence the name.

Kesik Minare

The citadel tower or **Hıdırlık Kulesi** ❺, dating from late antiquity, is a round tower on a square base. Originally part of the harbour fortifications, it was also probably used as a lighthouse. Directly behind the tower the extensive municipal park, ★ **Karaalioğlu Parkı** ❻, follows the coastline southwards. With its fountains, numerous tea gardens and fine promenades, this park is one of Antalya's greatest assets. About halfway up the hill a steep flight of steps leads down to a simple swimming pool between the rocks. A marvellous view extends along the coast from the promenades.

Family outing in the park

The palm-lined **Atatürk Boulevard** leads from the municipal park back into the town. On the left lie the remains of the old town wall, while on the right multi-storey blocks with modern shops overlook the busy road.

57

About halfway along stands ★ **Hadrian's Gate** ❼. It was built about AD130 to commemorate the visit of the Emperor Hadrian. The portal which is framed by two large towers consists of three wings and was originally finished in marble. Remains of the extravagantly sculpted mouldings have survived equally as well as the plaque on the left side. Some 2m (6ft) below the present ground level, earth furrowed by chariot wheels has been discovered. It is only possible to guess at what treasures lie buried here beneath the old town.

Hadrian's Gate

Hidden away at the end of the Atatürk Caddesi is a tiny alley called Eski Sebzeçiler, which is a paradise of Turkish cuisine. It marks the beginning of the **bazaar** ❽, a confusing maze of narrow lanes which extends as far as the bus station.

The ★★ **Archaeological Museum** ❾ in Antalya (Tuesday to Sunday 8.30am–12.30pm and 1.30–5pm) is one of the best of its type in Turkey. It displays finds ranging from prehistoric times up to the Ottoman years, including the amazing gallery of gods from Perge and some finely carved sarcophagi dating from the Roman era. The ethnographic section contains an exhibition about the Yörüken nomads.

Archaeological Museum, exhibit

The **Düden Falls**, a short distance outside the town, are certainly worth a visit. The Düden, one of many rivers that tumble from the Taurus mountains, descends in several stages. At the lower falls, the **Aşağı Düden Şelalesi**, just before Lara Beach to the east of the town, the river plunges

Pipes for sale in Antalya

well over 50m (160ft) into the sea. Boat trips run from the harbour along the coast to view the falls and often include a stop for bathing. The upper falls, the **Yukarı Düden Şelalesi**, 11km (7 miles) to the north, can be reached by taxi. The area is also popular with picnickers.

Termessos

Situated in an idyllic mountain region, ★★ **Termessos** (25km/16 miles) must be one of the prettiest destinations near the south coast. This ruined town which flourished during Roman times is situated at an altitude of about 1,000m (3,250ft) beneath the Güllük Dağı. Termessos is not a settlement of Greek origin like most of the ancient sites by the coast, but was first settled by a 'Barbarian people'. In this rough mountain terrain where pine trees cling to the steep slopes, the ruins of this 5th-century town remain almost as they were when an earthquake struck. A covering of dense undergrowth masks the pale stonework which remains untouched by archaeologists.

58

The Temple of Hadrian

A mountain track leads up to the site from a small museum by the road to Korkuteli. The remains of a **Temple of Hadrian** (2nd century AD) are visible in the car park. From here the King's Road leads to the oldest part of the town. At about the halfway point, the huge blocks of stone of the outer wall can be seen and the **gymnasium**, the athletes' training centre, stands on a long terrace directly behind the inner city gate. The long facade is so well preserved that it is hard to believe it was last used almost 1,500 years ago. Further on along the King's Road, past a completely overgrown colonnaded street, lies the **agora**, the public meeting place. Built above a huge substructure that was used as a cistern, it is bordered by lobbies and the bouleuterion (town hall). While the **Stoa of Attalos**, built in the 2nd century BC by Attalos II, the king of Pergamon, and the **Stoa of Osbaros** are badly overgrown, the **heroon** is worth close investigation. This sacred site carved out of the rock has niches in which the mythical founders of the city are portrayed. A little further on the right lies the **odeion** whose walls reach a good 10m (33ft) in height. It is surrounded by three **temples** which were dedicated to Artemis and Zeus.

The theatre has great views

On the left, a little further on, stands the ★ **theatre**, perhaps not as well preserved as the one at Aspendos (*see page 62*) but it occupies a much prettier spot. The view from the auditorium encompasses the steep mountains all around and on a clear day the sea is just visible behind them.

Up on the mountain lies the **necropolis**, the most interesting graveyard in the town with some marvellous carved sarcophagi. The stone covers have all been pulled off as if the Last Judgement has already taken place.

Excursion north of Antalya

Beyond Antalya and the Pamphylian plain, the Taurus mountains rise up. This is a relatively unexploited region where it is still possible to encounter the 'real' Turkey and where tourism is an unfamiliar concept. Seljuk caravanserais (*see page 65*) occur at regular distances – roughly a day's journey apart. One of the best preserved is **Suzuz Han** (70km/43 miles north of Antalya). It is impossible to miss its huge, richly decorated portal surrounded by tobacco fields.

Also on the route up to Burdur, is **Döşemealtı**, a famous carpet-weaving village. The woollen carpets, which have geometric patterns and a colour harmony of blues, dark greens and reds, are made by nomadic Yörük tribesmen who inhabit the Taurus Mountains.

Geometric patterns predominate

Burdur (127km/78 miles; pop. 56,000) is a provincial town which has grown rapidly in recent years. It stands on a hill above a lake of the same name (with a bathing beach). Every Friday a large market is held in the old town near the 14th-century Ulu Cami. Neolithic and Phrygian exhibits are displayed in the town's small museum. Explorers will discover one or two Ottoman houses that have been faithfully restored.

İsparta (148km/91 miles; pop. 110,000) has acquired a reputation for itself as a centre for the collection of rose essence. The dogrose is in blossom in May and June. Anyone thinking of buying a carpet will find that the prices here are more favourable than by the coast.

Eğirdir (182km/112 miles; pop. 17,000) is a pretty town with distinctive Oriental atmosphere by the side of Eğirdir lake. The old Seljuk fortress makes a picturesque sight. It is located on a peninsula at the tip of the town. The local inhabitants earn their living from fishing in the lake and from the extensive fruit orchards in the region.

59

İsparta mosque

A quality specimen

Route 6

The Turkish Riviera

From Antalya to Alanya via Side (134km/83 miles) *See map on pages 48–9*

Smile from the countryside

To the east of Antalya lies a wide and fertile plain, known in antiquity as Pamphylia. Now cotton fields and greenhouses characterise this, the most productive region of Turkey. The road follows a straight course through the countryside, with side roads running down to the sea. Many of the beaches of the Turkish riviera, set against the Taurus mountain backdrop, are irresistible. Over 2,500 years ago a number of these flat-topped mountains were occupied by Greek colonies and some splendid Roman buildings and Seljuk caravanserais lie hidden away in the hinterland. All of these attractions can easily be visited in one day from Antalya and the resorts of Side, İncekum and Alanya. The route itself will take two days.

About 18km (11 miles) beyond Antalya near the small town of **Aksu**, a road branches off to Perge passing a carpet weaving factory and an onyx studio.

Famed for its shrine to Artemis Pergaia, ★★ **Perge** (21km/13 miles) flourished during the Roman era. Pilgrims from all over Asia Minor came to visit the shrine, but the apostle Paul was also a visitor to the city and after his first journey, a Christian community became established here. By the 5th century, Perge was a bishopric with three large basilica. Like many other ancient towns, its decline was accelerated by silt deposits on the coast and it was finally abandoned before the end of the first millennium AD.

Roman gate and colonnaded street at Perge

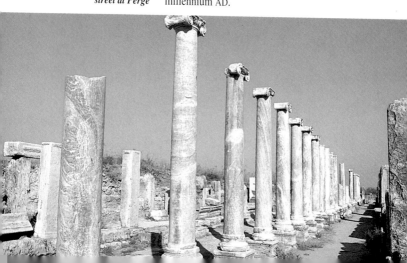

Although not the biggest in Pamphylia the second-century Roman ★ **amphitheatre** could accommodate as many as 14,000 spectators. The **relief frieze** from the stage house showing mythological scenes (currently undergoing restoration) has survived and is in very good condition. The **stadium**, one of the best preserved in all of the eastern Mediterranean, had seating for 12,000. Some marble friezes are displayed on the running track.

The entrance from the car park leads past the stadium and through what was the main gate. The angular **Roman gate** is decorated with splendid reliefs on the side facing the town. **Baths**, the agora and an older Hellenistic gate border the next square. The **south gate** with its two tall round towers was converted into a heroes square in the 2nd century AD. In the niches stand statues of the mythical founders of the city and some grand male figures. One of the statues shows Plancia Magna, a famous Artemis priestess. The square, surrounded by colonnades, was the **agora**, Perge's market place and main public assembly point. Shops were situated behind the columns and in the rear left-hand corner of the square an ancient **game board** can be seen.

Ancient inscription

A 200-m (220-yd) **colonnaded road** runs from the Hellenistic gate through the heart of the city to the acropolis. In the middle a water channel separates the 'traffic lanes', while the pavements ran under the shade of the columns. Part of the mosaic flooring can still be seen and on three columns there are reliefs of deities.

Further on, another – as yet unexcavated – colonnaded road crosses at right angles. This road ends near a **nymphaion** beneath the **acropolis** hill where only a few scanty relics remain. By the three-storey fountain house, certainly one of the most striking sights in the town, a reclining figure, the god Kestros, embodies the nearby river (then known as Kestros, now Aksu Çayı).

The nymphaion

The humpback bridge beyond **Serik** (21km/13 miles) was built by the Seljuks for their caravans. Take the turning here to Aspendos (41km/26 miles).

According to mythology, ★★ **Aspendos** was founded about 1000BC by Argolian Greeks under the leadership of the diviner Mopsos. In the 5th century BC Aspendos, which lay on the at that time navigable Eurymedon (now Köprü Çayı) and was the most important port in the region, became the principal town in Pamphylia and also seat of the Persian governor. In 190BC the city came under Roman control and subsequently enjoyed a period of great prosperity, to such an extent that it became a victim of the avaricious and exploitative proconsul Verres who was condemned by Cicero in a famous speech. Aspendos later lost its important role within Pamphylia to Perge, but it

Theatregoers in Aspendos

The theatre and aqueduct

remained inhabited at least until the Seljuk era as they used the theatre as a caravanserai.

Although it was restored during the 1950s the ★★ **theatre** at Aspendos is in extraordinarily good condition, and the Seljuks also deserve some credit. According to an inscription above the entrance, the arena with seating for 20,000 people was built for Marcus Aurelius in AD170. Despite certain Greek features such as its hillside auditorium and its more than semi-circular form, it is an excellent example of a Roman theatre. The **facade** above the orchestra which used to be covered with marble cladding, friezes, gables and statues is most impressive. One or two diamond-shaped bricks originated from the Seljuks. Another remarkable feature is the acoustics: coins jingling in the orchestra can be heard way up in the gallery. The **chambers** for the senior dignitaries above the right-hand box are of interest as is the museum in the stage house (open 8am–7pm in summer, otherwise 8am–5.30pm). It contains displays of masks and coins.

The remains of the **acropolis** behind the theatre extend around a huge **agora**. Worth investigating are the **town hall** (bouleuterion), an 80-m (260-ft) long **basilica** which was used as a market hall, as well as a **nymphaion** with a splendid, but slightly askew facade opening onto the square. Make a detour across the hill to the north east to examine the remains of a Roman **aqueduct**, which used to carry water to the acropolis.

A detour to the ancient ruined site at Selge (about 50km/30 miles) will take a morning (take the turning near **Taşağıl**). The road goes deep into the Taurus mountains, through dense pine forests but always following the course of the Köprü Çayı, which in spring flows freely down to the sea. A trout restaurant is situated alongside the river just

Lunch by the river

beyond **Beşkonak** and canoes and inflatable dinghies can be hired here during the summer.

★★ **Selge** is now the principal – and probably the only – asset as far as the inhabitants of the farming hamlet of Altınkaya are concerned. Like Termessos, Selge belonged to the Pisidians, but given its remote position at an altitude of about 1,000m (3,250ft), it enjoyed a degree of independence during the years of Roman rule. During the Byzantine era it was the seat of a bishop. While it is easy to make out the **theatre** from a distance, many of the other ruins are hidden among the houses. To the south of the theatre was the stadium and at one end stood the town's main gate. Traces of a **colonnade**, an **agora** and a **monastery** can be found on the hill above it.

Side

No one can fail to notice that ★★ **Side** (84km/52 miles; pop. 2,000) lies ahead. Roadside signs written in large letters inform visitors about the town's 70 jewellers. Is Side just one big shopping centre?. Well, yes and no. The town, which has a history going back 2,500 years, successfully manages to link holiday souvenir hunting and commerce with some interesting Roman buildings. In addition, the hotels by the long sandy beaches to both east and west can meet most holidaymakers' needs. Sporting facilities range from paragliding to horse-riding.

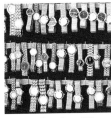

Watches for sale at Side

Side has long, sandy beaches

Ancient Side was originally a Greek colony, but from the 2nd century BC it rose under Roman protection to become one of the most important commercial cities on the south coast. Around 130BC it was used as a base by Cilician pirates but, after the Roman general Pompeius had brought order back to the seas, Side's prosperity revived in the 2nd and 3rd centuries AD. Lawlessness returned in the 9th century with bands of Arabs plundering the city on a number of occasions. It was the beginning of the 20th century before Side was resettled, this time by Turkish fishermen who had been expelled from Crete. It remained a small fishing village until well into the 1970s, but then tourism arrived with a vengeance. Hotels sprang up almost overnight and the character of the town changed dramatically. The hotels grew taller and more and more houses were turned into shops and restaurants. As a consolation, the Temple of Apollo was beautifully restored.

The road from the main highway to the town passes along the remains of an **aqueduct.** If the car park in the town is full, then traffic is diverted elsewhere and passengers ferried into the town by a tractor bus. Just beyond the barrier stood the **great gate [A]** but little remains of it today. The main colonnaded thoroughfare runs southwest and the column stumps can still be identified.

It's best to start a tour of the town near the **theatre [B]**. This dates from after the birth of Christ and is one

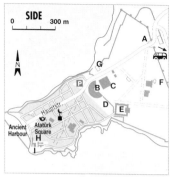

Hero from the past

Camels get everywhere

The Manavgat falls

of the few theatres in Asia Minor that is not built on a slope, but is free-standing in true Roman style. The rows of seats, which could accommodate as many as 14,000 spectators, rest on huge supports and most of these are still in excellent condition. However, the stage house has collapsed and the marble decorative work has been transferred to the agora. In the **agora [C]**, originally surrounded by rows of columns, one of the most famous slave markets in antiquity was held. Halls, some 7m (22ft) high and each with 25 columns, provided shade, while in the middle stood the **Temple of Tyche**, the goddess of fate. It is only a few steps from here along the **Byzantine town wall [D]** to the **library [E]**. The latter consisted of three rooms, but now only one wall with statue niches survives. The imposing **Hellenistic town wall [F]** can also be reached from the beach.

The ★★ **Archaeological Museum [G]** opposite the agora (daily 8am–noon and 1.30–5.30pm) is housed in the ancient baths. Displays include decorative sculptures, statues and artefacts discovered during the excavations. It is practically impossible to miss the harbour. The main shopping street with carpet warehouses, restaurants and fur shops leads straight to the waterfront. The ancient **harbour**, which is now silted up, used to occupy the land between the present-day post office and the Mergiz restaurant. A promenade runs from where today's fishing and pleasure boats moor to the ★ **Temple of Apollo [H]** with its five restored columns and a section of gable. The **Temple of Artemis [I]** directly adjacent and the *tholos* dedicated to the Anatolian moon god Men look rather neglected in comparison, as do the other ancient ruins around the bazaar.

Manavgat, a lively town on the banks of the river Manavgat, has some pleasant restaurants. Saturday is market day and the best day for a visit. Three kilometres (2 miles) further north lies **Manavgat Şelalesi**. The falls here attract both picnickers and swimmers. There are a number of trout restaurants by the **Oymapınar reservoir** a little further north. On the return journey it is worth paying a visit to the ancient town of **Seleukia** (or Lyrbe) where ruins surround a levelled-off agora.

İncekum meaning 'fine sand' is the name given to the long section of beach which stretches eastward from Side as far as Konaklı. **Club Ali Bey** housed in delightful Ottoman style premises is generally regarded as one of the best hotels in Turkey and **İncekum Parkı** is worth a visit for its luxuriant subtropical vegetation and variety of organised beach activities.

★★ **Alara Han** (turning near **Yeşilköy**) is a fortified caravanserai, one of the many built by the Seljuks in Anatolia during the 13th century. It is also one of the best preserved on the south coast. The Seljuks built their caravanserais about a day's journey apart. The Turkic Seljuks overran Asia Minor and ruled Anatolia from their capital, Konya. Trade, interrupted by constant skirmishes between the Turks and the Byzantines in which the Crusaders also had a hand, began to pick up only after the Seljuks under Alacddin Keykubat I had conquered the coastal regions. Another important factor was a new form of transport which had appeared in Anatolia: the camel.

Sultan Keykubat had the Alara Han built around 1230 after he had gained control of the older Byzantine castle on the hill to the north. The fortress-like caravanserai with its high entrance portal, a typical Seljuk feature, was intended as a night camp and feeding station and it also offered protection from bandits.

The complex is grouped around an inner courtyard with bedrooms and kitchen; *hamam* (baths), a small mosque and a guardroom are situated alongside the forecourt. Two large gates lead from the forecourt into the large rooms running around the inner courtyard where the beasts of burden were kept. The animals could be observed through slits in the wall.

Alanya

Beyond İncekum, the foothills of the Taurus mountains come down close to the sea. Bananas grow on the hillsides and farmers offer them for sale at the roadside. Suddenly a rocky peninsula, jutting out into the sea and crowned by a long crenellated fortress, appears in the distance. ★★ **Alanya** (134km/83 miles; pop. 60,000), a city with many hotels and modern buildings extends along the nar-

The old harbour at Alanya

Alara Han

Bananas ripen near Alanya

row coastal plain, resting at the foot of the peninsula. It is a busy centre with some fine beaches and a place where the Turkish and Oriental atmosphere has not been affected by the onset of tourism.

Alanya (or Korakesion as it was known in antiquity) was a border town between Pamphylia and 'wild Cilicia'. It occupied an almost impregnable position and was thus relatively easy to defend in turbulent times. About 140BC the town was the headquarters of the notorious Cilician pirates whose antics were brought to a conclusion by Pompeius in 67BC. Just under 40 years later, Mark Anthony presented the fortress to his lover Cleopatra. Alanya enjoyed its greatest prosperity after the Seljuk Alaeddin Keykubat established his winter residence in the town. Alanya acquired not only its name from this sultan but also most of its grand buildings.

The **bazaar** with shops, tea houses and restaurants lies between the main thoroughfare and the harbour to the east of the citadel.

The Red Tower

★ **Kızıl Kule**, the 'Red Tower' by the harbour, is the biggest building in the town's fortifications. It was completed in 1228 and now houses the **Ethnographic Museum** (Tuesday to Sunday 8am–noon and 1.30–5.30pm). Boats leave from here for the ★★ **Seljuk dockyard** (Tersane) at the foot of the citadel. Five vaulted galleries measuring 7 x 42m (22 x 138ft) are linked by pointed arches. The phosphorus cave where light is reflected in the gleaming green water is also worth a visit.

The local vernacular

A walk up to the **citadel** is an interesting, but strenuous activity. Another option is to take a taxi or bus, which leave from outside the Kuyularönü mosque. Pretty wooden houses and the main gate to old Alanya are situated at a lower level. At the summit **Iç Kale** and its battlemented wall provide a splendid view of the lower town, a worthwhile reward after the arduous ascent. Little remains of the interior apart from a small Byzantine church. **Adam Atacaği**, where executions took place, is an eerie spot. The condemned were simply hurled into the sea. But they had just one chance of survival: if they threw a stone and it reached the water, they were reprieved. More Seljuk and Turkish buildings, including the **Suleyman Mosque** and the rather inaccessible **Ehmedek Fortress**, are situated to the north of Iç Kale.

The Egyptian queen Cleopatra has given her name to two beaches. One of them is a small bay which is said by some to have been linked with the fortress by a tunnel and which can only be reached by boat. The other Cleopatra beach, a beautiful sandy stretch, lies to the west. The nearby **Archaeological Museum** (Tuesday to Sunday 9am–noon and 1.30–5.30pm) displays finds from antiquity and its ethnographic section is also of interest.

Museum exhibit

If it gets too hot on the beach, then head for **Damlataş Cave**. Noted for its huge stalagmites, the temperature within remains at a constant 22°C (71°F), an environment believed to be beneficial for those suffering from asthma and other respiratory diseases, although elderly people with heart ailments should avoid it.

Although silk scarves are something of a rarity now, they are still much in demand. The women of Alanya sell them on the citadel hill together with embroidery. Business is not too good as most holidaymakers drive up the hill in their cars and do not bother to wander through old Alanya. Also, the silk is rather coarse, not quite how most people imagine the lightest material in the world to be.

Silk scarves for sale

But there is a long tradition of silk-making in Alanya. Travellers on the old Silk Road are said to have smuggled silkworms out of China in walking sticks as early as Byzantine times. The silkworms thrive in the hot but damp climate on the Turkish south coast and, in 16th-century Europe, silk was one of Turkey's most sought after export products. Many of the villages around Alanya still raise silkworms, but the demand for the fibre comes from carpet weavers.

Shirts are also in demand   **67**

Obtaining the raw silk is a painstaking process. The female butterfly (*bombyx mori*) lays about 400 eggs on the leaf of a mulberry tree. The silkworms hatch at temperatures between 15 and 30°C (60 and 86°F) and then, after gorging themselves on the leaves, spin a cocoon about 4cm (1½ inches) long. The creatures are killed by immersion in boiling water, which also softens the cocoon so that the delicate filament can be unwound – a process that is still usually carried out by hand. The women then weave shawls from the silk thread and use plant dyes to colour them making it a genuinely natural product.

Coastal contrast near Alanya

Route 7

From pine forests to cotton field country

From Alanya to Antakya via Adana (615km/381 miles)

Adana shoeshine
Roman mosaics at Antakya

Just out of Alanya, the coast road starts to climb the steep hillsides of the Taurus mountains. 'Wild Cilicia' as it was known in antiquity is for experienced travellers who are not frightened of breathtaking hairpin bends and will appreciate the austere beauty of the landscape. After dense forest comes 'flat Cilicia' and the Çukorova plain, one of Turkey's most intensively farmed regions. The scenery is not especially attractive but a number of ancient sites and medieval castles can be found around the major city of Adana. In Antakya, our final destination, the museum of Roman mosaics is certainly worth a visit. Allow six days for this tour.

Bananas are cultivated on the narrow terraces which run to the east of Alanya (*see pages 65–7*). **Iotape** (35km/22 miles) was a Roman port, named by Antiochus IV of Commagene after his daughter. The sparse ruins are hardly worth a closer look, but the small bays between the rocks can boast water which is considerable cleaner than the Bay of Alanya. **Gazipaşa** (47km/29 miles) lies amid monot-

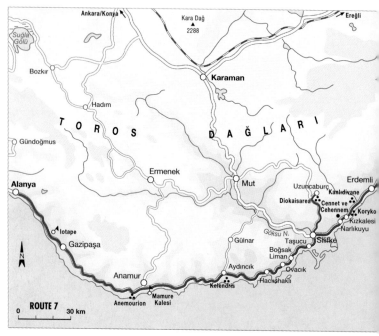

onous fields and has little to commend it. There is an isolated sandy beach (only camp-sites) and the **ruins** of ancient Selinus, where the Roman emperor Trajan died in AD117. Beyond Gazipaşa the dizzying climb over the mountain sides begins. Not even the most experienced drivers will enjoy the prospect of a steep drop down to the sea on the right and lorries and cars approaching at speed on the left!

Anamur (120km/74 miles; pop. 38,000) occupies the centre of a small plain surrounded by mountains. This farming town with its lively Wednesday market is situated away from the coast, but a small holiday village has grown up by the long sandy beach (4km/2½ miles). The name of the town is derived from ancient **Anemourion**, now an extensive ruined site at the cape. On the summit of one of the foothills stands a **castle** built by a Lesser Armenian prince (12th century) and in the town itself there is a Byzantine **town wall**, a large **bath-house,** an **odeion**, the remains of a **theatre** and a towering **apse** from a church that was never completed.

Anemourion

★★ **Mamure Kalesi**, a 12th-century fortress, is by far the finest castle on the south coast. The walls, almost completely intact, follow the coast, but are dominated by a keep and a large watch-tower. The emirs of Karaman later built a mosque in the courtyard. It is possible to

The mosque in Mamure Kalesi

69

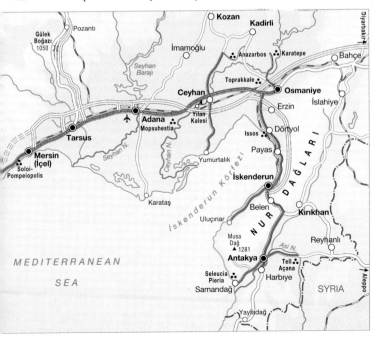

Afternoon tea in Silifke
The Lesser Armenian castle

climb the watch-tower and explore the (unsecured) curtain wall, but a good head for heights is required.

The stretch of road from Anamur to Silifke does not hug the coast. There are some idyllic bays, many of them popular with Turkish holidaymakers. Campers in search of peace and quiet will enjoy the sleepy villages of **Sipahılı** and **Hacıishaklı** and their isolated beaches. **Boğsak Liman**, on the other hand, is a livelier spot with several hotels and the small port of **Taşucu** is also fairly busy in the summer, but the water is none too clean. Among the remains of ancient **Kelendris** in **Aydıncık** is a well-preserved Roman house-tomb.

Silifke (264km/163 miles; 45,000), a small provincial town in the shadow of a Lesser Armenian castle, has a distinguished history but little to show for it. Founded by Seleukos Nikator, one of Alexander the Great's generals and the first king of one of the strongest Hellenistic empires, Seleukia ad Kalykadnos was the former capital of 'wild Cilicia'. The last column of a large Temple of Jupiter and the artefacts displayed in the **Archaeological Museum** are among the few reminders of these times. In the Byzantine era, after the martyrdom of St Thekla, a disciple of the apostle Paul, the town became an important place of pilgrimage. A crypt and the apse of a church over 80m (260ft) long in what is now **Ayatekla** (5km/3 miles) are all that remain of this sacred spot. Up in the mountains by the side of a river, a plaque records the place where in 1190, during the Third Crusade, the Emperor Frederick Barbarossa drowned while bathing.

The ancient shrine of ★★ **Olba Diocaesarea** near the village of Uzuncaburç is situated in magnificent mountain woodland at an altitude of 1,100m (3,600ft). This site was also founded by Seleukos and, in Hellenistic times, was the seat of the Teukrid priest kings who ruled western Cilicia. It is interesting to observe modern Turkish village life continuing around the almost completely preserved columns of the **Temple of Zeus**, which was later converted into a church. Huts have even been erected on the rows of seating in the theatre auditorium. A **colonnade**, a triple-arched **gate** and a huge **watch-tower** appear among the village houses.

The mosaic at Narlıkuyu

Beyond Silifke on the coast road is **Narlıkuyu**, where the remains of a mosaic are visible in the ancient baths and fish restaurants overlook the shore. The ★ **Cennet ve Cehennen** (Heaven and Hell) caves are worth making the 3-km (2-mile) detour. Known collectively as the Corycian caves, these two sink-holes have, since the earliest times, been perceived as a devil's lair. The Greeks thought that the snake-headed god Typhon, who had been vanquished by Zeus, had hidden away in the inaccessible 'hell' cave.

A temple was built on the edge of the larger cave in his honour and this can be reached via a long flight of steps. In Christian times, a church was also built here as a symbol of victory over the underworld. Turkish pilgrims still come here to seek guidance from the spirits.

The 'Heaven and Hell' caves...

...a devil's lair

★ **Kızkalesi** (290km/179 miles; pop. 500) is a pretty holiday village by the beach of ancient **Korykos**. For those who would prefer to give the major city of Adana a miss, then the Çukurova plain and even Antakya can be reached on day trips. The holiday infrastructure is good (hotels, restaurants, watersports and diving) and the beach has lovely sand and a few rocks.

The two medieval ★ **castles** are of interest: one stands on an offshore island and was built by the Byzantines at the beginning of the 12th century; the mainland castle is older and may well date from the 4th century. In the 13th century the stronghold was captured by the Lesser Armenian army of Hethum I (1226–69). Both castles were strengthened and enlarged to their present form. During the Crusader years, Korykos was an important staging post for travellers to the Holy Land and it stayed in Christian hands until 1448, when it fell to the Turkish emirs of Karaman. On the seaward side of the land castle, a Roman **gate** can still be identified and other ancient remains are situated around the necropolis. Some richly decorated sarcophagi have survived and these can be seen by the **sacred way** directly above the land castle.

Castle ruins

A number of small beaches lie to the right, within a short distance of the main road east. The jumble of ruins that were once ancient **Elaiussa-Sebaste** are situated on the left. A basilica by a deep karst sink-hole, a Hellenistic watch-tower and a number of tombs remain from ancient **Kanytelis** near Kanlıdivane. From **Erdemli** (326km/202 miles) onwards, the coast is lined with Turkish holiday villages – some with 10-storey tower blocks.

Refreshments in Mersin

Mersin (353km/218 miles; pop. 450,000), a modern town founded in the middle of the 19th century, marks the beginning of the broad Çukorova plain. It offers little to tourists, apart from the **Luna Parkı** by the palm-lined coast road. Drinks sellers in the bazaar, situated between the Kordon and İstiklal Caddesi, offer a purplish drink called *aşlama*. *Simit* sellers balance their trays of sesame rings on their heads.

The modern face of Tarsus

For centuries **Tarsus** (380km/235 miles) has been the capital of Cilicia: the Hittites built a castle in the 15th century BC, a university was founded during the Hellenistic years, Saul, better known as the apostle Paul, was born here, Julian Apostata the last rationalist in antiquity died here, the capital of the Lesser Armenian empire was based here...but all that is in the past and gone for good. Apart from the **Cleopatra Gate** through which the Egyptian queen is said to have entered the town in order to ensnare Mark Anthony, there is nothing else to be seen. The district around the **Ulu Cami**, which was built in 1385 on the foundations of the famous Byzantine Hagia Sophia, is the bustling and colourful heart of the city, while alongside the great mosque, a market is held daily in the ★ **Kırkkaşık Carsısı** (the forty-spoon market).

Adana – centre for the southeast

Adana (420km/260 miles; pop. 1.1 million) has only recently become the fourth Turkish city to have a million inhabitants. A settlement has existed here for many hundreds of years but it has nearly always been overshadowed by nearby Tarsus. The town's fortunes improved in the middle of the 19th century when the sultan sold the land to Armenians who set about developing the huge cereal and cotton plantations on the surrounding marshland. During World War II the Armenians were expelled as part of a bloody episode and the land was retaken by the Turks. With seasonal workers obliged to work under semi-feudal conditions, the Turkish landowners soon found themselves very rich. Adana is now the cosmopolitan centre for the southeast of the country.

Adana's ★★ **Archaeological Museum** is certainly worth a visit. Displays include artefacts from the late Hittite palace at Karatepe and the magnificent Achilleus sarcophagus with carvings showing scenes from the Trojan war. The old town is situated by the Seyhan river where a **Roman bridge** and the early 16th-century **Ulu Cami** (mausolea of the Ramazan emirs) on Kizilay Caddesi bear witness to the city's historic past. Behind the unusual **clock tower** lies Adana's bustling ★ **bazaar**, which is noted for its copperware.

Emirs' tombs in the Ulu Cami

Although **Karataş** (60km/37 miles) – beyond a wide plain of monotonous cereal and cotton plantations – is a summer resort for Adana's residents, its polluted beaches are not recommended.

Karataş is the local resort

Yilanlıkale (Snakes' Castle), a Lesser Armenian fortification and a Hittite relief of King Muwatallis near **Sirkeli** (*see page 77*) are situated to the east of Adana, on the stretch of road before the provincial town of **Ceyhan**.

Yumurtalık (180km/111 miles from Adana), known in the Middle Ages as Lajazzo, was a Christian stronghold occupied first by Genoese traders and later by Lesser Armenians. A broad bay extends to the east of the **castle** by the harbour.

Anazarbos was the name of an ancient site to the north of Ceyhan. It is now known as Dilekkaya (75km/46 miles from Adana). Given encouragement by Augustus and then elevated to capital of eastern Cilicia by the Severan dynasty, Anazarbos fell into Arab hands in 796. Given its almost impregnable position, the fortress here was later much contested and eventually became one of the main Lesser Armenian castles. On the flat plain beneath the citadel stands an **arch** dating from the time of Septimius Severinus. The **castle** 200m (625ft) higher is better preserved. Various lines of fortification remain, together with a ruined church. The castle offers a commanding view of the ancient town.

73

A local falconer

Outside **Osmaniye** (90km/56 miles from Adana), the main road comes close to **Toprakkale**, another castle in this much disputed region. A detour to the north will take in the ★ **Karatepe National Park** where just under 3,000 years ago the palace of the late-Hittite King Asitawanda once stood. Among the remains are gates with lion figures

Evening near Toprakkale

Fishing at İskenderun

Ulucınar

and animal reliefs. Just after the coast road turns south, it passes the plain to the west of **Dörtyol** where in 333 Alexander the Great won the famous battle of Issos. Take a detour from **Payas** to **Sokullu Mechmed Paşa Külliye** (1574), a large complex founded by the Grand Vizier that comprises a mosque (still in use) and a huge, abandoned caravanserai. A Genoese castle known as Cinkale (Castle of the Spirits) stands on an offshore island.

İskenderun (586km/363 miles) was the first town founded by Alexander the Great during his successful campaign against the Persians, but it reveals little of its past. Modern buildings and wide streets dominate the townscape and container ships and naval vessels occupy most of the berths in the port. Kebab stands and a few *lokantalar* around the **Ulu Cami** help to give the old town a distinctive Turkish atmosphere. A municipal park by the **coast road** contains a children's playground, tea gardens and a disco.

The **Arsuz**, a medium-category hotel in the small seaside resort of **Ulucınar** (33km/21 miles from İskenderun), offers the best accommodation in the region.

Continue towards the south, taking the Belen pass over the rugged **Nur Dağları** mountains (1,940m/6,363ft). This mountain range forms the border with Syria. In the village of **Belen**, pay a visit to the **Süleymaniye Han**, a caravanserai built during the rule of Sultan Süleyman. It is now a stylish place to take tea. The Asi Nehri plain and the Antakya hinterland are visible from the other side of the mountain ridge.

Antakya

Antakya: pistachio seller

★ **Antakya** (606km/375 miles), or Hatay, was known in Hellenistic times as Antioch. It was the capital of the powerful Seleukid empire, the town of the first Christians and, after Alexandria, one of the cultural centres for the Roman Eastern empire and the early Byzantine empire. It was overrun by Arabs in 638 and later occupied by the Seljuks. For a time it was the capital of a principality of European Crusaders, but in 1269 it fell to the Egyptian Mamelukes. After World War I Antakya was occupied by French forces, who returned it to the Turks after a plebiscite in 1939, thereby securing the support of Turkey in the approaching war with Hitler's Germany.

Evidence from the town's past can be seen in the splendid ★★ **Hatay Müsesi** (daily except Monday 9am–noon and 1.30–5pm). This museum is renowned worldwide for its collection of Roman mosaics. Most of these huge floor decorations were found in private homes in Tarsus, Seleucia Pieria and Daphne. They mainly depict hunting scenes or illustrate the ancient myths. **Sen Piyer Kilise**, a few miles out of the town in the direction of Reyhanlı,

Roman mosaics, Hatay Müsesi

Mixed grill
Grotto of St Peter, detail

is worth a visit. The **Grotto of St Peter** was founded by the first Christians and Paul is said to have preached here. The Moorish-looking porch was added by the Crusaders. The castle on the hill above the town also dates from the Crusader era.

75

Excursions from Antakya

Samandağ (27km/16 miles from Antakya) is a typically Arab provincial town, most of whose inhabitants are Alevites (*see page 10*); however, as in Antakya, a number of Syrian Orthodox Christians still live in the town. The Shrine of the Prophet Hizir (a contemporary of Moses), who is worshipped by the Alevites stands about 5km (3 miles) from the town centre beside a badly polluted beach.

Seleucia Pieria some 4km (2½ miles) towards Çevlik was the first capital of the Seleukids and later the port for Antioch. As well as a number of interesting rock tombs, one of the Roman empire's finest aqueducts has survived here. The **Titus Canal** is another grand engineering project. Measuring 1.3km (¾ mile) in length, 6m (20ft) wide and 5m (16ft) high, it was built under the Emperor Titus by Jewish prisoners of war in order to protect the harbour from flooding.

Harbiye (8km/5 miles from Antakya), formerly known as Daphne, was an affluent villa suburb for Antioch. The area, dotted with oaks and cypresses, descends in terraces down to the valley where tiny streams merge to form a large waterfall. Few buildings of interest remain, but the picnic park makes a refreshing spot for anyone trying to escape the oppressive sultry atmosphere in the summer.

The waterfall at Harbiye

Alalah, near **Tell Açana** (23km/14 miles), was the palace of the Assyrian King Jarimlim (1750BC). Sections of town wall with a lion gate and the foundations are all that remain of this monument from the ancient Mesopotamian civilisation.

Art History

Opposite: Temple of Artemis at Side

The Turkish Mediterranean coast still bears witness to the many different civilisations which once inhabited Asia Minor – from the Hittite relief dating from the middle of the 2nd millennium BC to the modern Turkish mosque.

Antalya Museum exhibit

Prehistory and the early empires

Finds discovered in Neanderthal caves near Karain north of Antalya demonstrate clearly the importance of Asia Minor in prehistory. A Copper Age settlement near Mersin has been discovered and the earliest remains at Troy go back to the Bronze Age. Clearly, the techniques of animal domestication, land cultivation and metalworking reached Europe via Asia Minor.

Hittites

The Hittites, an Indo-Germanic race who originated from western Asia, ruled almost all of Asia Minor during the middle of the 2nd millennium BC. Their capital Hattuşa lay to the east of Ankara. Rock reliefs by the coast, eg near Manisa, near Karabel to the east of İzmir and near Sirkeli on the Ceyhan to the east of Adana, are the work of Hittite masons and a palace dating from the later Hittite era (c 800BC) has been uncovered on the Karatepe north of Osmaniye. The reliefs and sculptures that have survived are displayed in the museum at Adana and they document the advanced artistic achievements of this ancient tribe. The first example of writing in Asia Minor can be seen on the clay tablets which contain astonishing evidence of the Hittite civilisation, such as political treaties and military conflicts and details about other tribes.

Phrygians and Lydians

Only burial offerings and pottery remain from these tribes, who survived until the Persian invasions of the 6th century BC. The Lydians under King Alyattes and the legendary Croesus were the first peoples to mint coins and are therefore said to have invented money. The Lydians were conquered by the Persians in 546BC and they controlled the whole of Asia Minor until 336. Little remains of their civilisation apart from a few small finds such as seals, coins and jewellery.

Lycians

The Lycians settled along the Mediterranean coast between Fethiye and Antalya. Many mysteries surround this tribe who, like the Greeks, were town dwellers. A number of their tombs have survived (*see pages 50–2*). The Lycians enjoyed their greatest prosperity in the 5th and 4th centuries BC after they came under the influence of the Greeks.

Lycian keel sarcophagus, Fethiye

Carians

Equally little is known about the Carians who settled in the region around Muğla on the Aegean coast. Their writings have still not been deciphered. After the decline of the Mycenean culture, the Carians settled on some of the islands in the eastern Aegean, but none of their buildings from the earlier period have been found. The tomb of a Carian queen has recently been discovered near Bodrum and the finds are now on display in Bodrum castle. Bodrum itself, formerly known as Halikarnassos, is the site of the Carians' best known monument, the burial temple of the Persian satrap Mausolos – one of the seven wonders of the ancient world.

Greeks

As early as the 10th century BC, the Greeks established colonies on the Aegean coast (Aeolians and Ionians) and Dorians settled along the Mediterranean coast during the 8th century BC. Maritime travel brought the Greeks into contact with Oriental influences (Assyrians, Phoenicians, Egyptians) which are clearly visible in Greek art. While nothing more than foundation walls remain from the Archaic period (700–500BC) or the Classical period (500–mid-4th century BC), the Hellenistic era, when Alexander the Great's vast empire brought Greek and Oriental civilisations together (350–100BC), is better documented. During these years Miletus and Priene were built. The Pergamon Altar shows better than anything else the extent of the Greeks' artistic skills. Other examples of buildings from this period can be found in Knidos near Marmaris, Didyma, Diocaesarea/Olba and Silifke.

Detail from the temple at Didyma

Romans

The majority of ancient remains along the coast of Asia Minor are Roman. In the first two centuries after the birth of Christ, the people of the Mediterranean basin enjoyed the benefits of the *Pax Romana*, the Roman peace. Fine colonnaded streets and monumental theatres, aqueducts and baths were built. A network of roads opened up the land – some bridges built by Roman engineers are still in use. Many fine structures remain in Pergamon, Ephesus, Miletus, Aphrodisias, Hierapolis, Side, Aspendos and Termessos.

The Roman bridge at Silifke

Temple of Aphrodite, Aphrodisias

Byzantines

Few Byzantine remains have survived along the Turkish Mediterranean coast. Fortifications built to protect the citizens from Arab, Persian and Turkish attacks, and some ruined basilica are the principal surviving legacies of this era. Many fine structures were built during the reign of the Emperor Justinian and the partially-reconstructed Basil-

ica of St John in modern Selçuk is one of the best examples. Many castles date from the late Byzantine era such as those in Bodrum, Simena near Kaş, Anamur and Korykos near Silifke, but in many cases these were built by Crusaders. With the arrival of the Crusaders, European influence along the south coast of Asia Minor grew. From their headquarters on the island of Rhodes the Knights of St John controlled the coastline as far as Cyprus until well into the 16th century. In the 11th century Armenians occupied the plain around Adana (*see page 9*) and many of the castles they built have survived to this day.

St John's Basilica, Selçuk

Turks

Well before the end of the 1st millennium AD tribes of Turkic nomads from Central Asia began moving west in search of better pastures and water. Ancient historians called them the 'scourge of God' and were terrified. But the Turks were not savages. Semi-nomadic, they cultivated land, raised animals and worshipped their own god of the heavens, *Sky Tengrı*. In the 8th century they adopted Islam as their faith and fought as mercenaries for the Caliph of Baghdad.

79

Seljuks

From 1071 the Seljuks – not a tribe, but a dynasty – ruled large parts of Asia Minor. Their power base was Konya in central Anatolia and from here, up until 1250, they conquered a number of coastal towns. Many Seljuk caravanserais noted for their splendid portals have survived as well as the Yivli Minare in Antalya and the citadel in Alanya. The Seljuks oversaw the fusion of Arabic and Oriental art with old Turkish traditions.

Ottomans

The Ottomans initially developed Seljuk art but after the conquest of Constantinople and the expansion of the empire, Byzantine, Persian, Slavic and Egyptian influences brought some new approaches. Under a system known as *devşirme*, Christian boys were brought to the sultan's court and trained as soldiers, architects and administrators while the Turkish nomads were cast into a secondary role. With domed mosques such as the Hagia Sophia in what was then Constantinople (now İstanbul), the Ottomans created architecture of world stature; however, there are no works of comparable grandeur on the coast. Only the Muradiye Mosque in Manisa with its famous İznik tiles stands out. Persian influences in the Ottoman years were responsible for the now traditional carpet patterns. Arabic-style calligraphy reached a high standard with an increasing tendency to the ornamental and examples of this can be seen in İzmir and Antalya.

Carpets show Persian influence

Modern Turkish Culture

The gap between popular and intellectual culture in Turkey has been bridged considerably in recent years with further democratisation and the lifting of economic restraints. Book stores abound carrying the latest translations of international writing, as well as modern Turkish writers, many formerly banned. In addition, there has been an upsurge of interest in historical writing and Ottoman authors. Film producers such as the well known, but previously banned Yılmaz Güney (*Yol, Suru*) are beginning to play a role in contemporary Turkey, although Hollywood imports, low-brow films and television series are immensely popular. Ever since Ottoman times, officialdom has viewed certain intellectuals, usually left-wing, with distrust, and even today censorship holds sway over matters relating to national security and sensitive political issues.

Contemporary icon

FATOŞ SEZGİ

The poet, Nazim Hikmet, who headed the list of proscribed writers even long after his death in the USSR in 1963, is gaining belated recognition. Yaşar Kemal, probably the best known Turkish author, has won literary prizes but currently faces serious charges relating to an allegedly anti-Turkish newspaper article. The left-wing satirist Aziz Nesin, who died in 1995, was also imprisoned for his writings. His publication of excerpts from Salman Rushdie's *Satanic Verses* triggered the massacre in Sivas by enraged fundamentalists in which forty writers died.

Writers such as Yaşar Kemal and Sait Faik (1906–54), concerned themselves with the everyday life of ordinary people. Faik wrote of craftsmen and tradesmen in Istanbul, and Kemal decried the lot of the peasant under the feudal despotism of the Ağas. Since 1970 the advent of women writers such as Adalet Ağaoğlu is significant in its contribution of domestic content to the modern Turkish novel. Latife Tekin Ferit Edgü and Aras Ören expose the problems of villagers migrating to the cities in search of work, life in the *gecekondu* and the uncertainty that comes when new ways threaten the old order. Orhan Pamuk, two of whose books are available in English as *The White Castle* and *The Black Book*, represents the new wave of postmodernist writing in Turkey.

The Turkish music scene is much more lively. Turkish pop, a mixture of Turkish/Oriental music and modern arrangements, is ever-present – on the bus, in the restaurants, on the beach or in the disco. Tarkan from İstanbul has had a number of successful 'summer hits', many of which are covers of Western songs, even opera, while Metin Şentürk, a promising newcomer, has produced some entertaining hits. But reading about music is no substitute for listening to the real thing.

Festivals and Folklore

Turkey is a country with a rich culture which stems partly from its Islamic faith and partly from the old nomadic traditions. Despite the modernisation programme and the impact of Westernisation, traditions continue to be carefully maintained.

The main festivals have a religious background: *Şeker Bayramı* or the Sugar Festival marks the end of Ramadan (in February) while the *Kurban Bayramı* (Holy Days of Sacrifice) is the most important Islamic festival (in April). Public life comes to a standstill and the festivities last for several days; however, the celebrations generally take place within the family.

Military parades and dance performances are held for four main national events (*see page 94*). The Day of the Child (23 April) and the Youth Day (19 May) are celebrated in almost every village. Children dress up in colourful Ottoman-style costumes and perform folk dances.

The *zeybek* dances, similar to the Greek rounds, are unique to the Mediterranean coast as are the *oyun* dances, such as the military-style *kılıç kalkan oyunu* (sabre and shield dance) and the *kaşık oyunları* (spoon dance). The best known Turkish dance is, of course, the belly dance, which is said to have originated in Egypt. Traditional instruments such as the big *davul* drum and the *zurna,* a chirping conical oboe, are not only used to accompany the dances but also weddings and circumcision ceremonies.

Family celebrations

End of March: Mesir festival in Manisa. Sweets are thrown into the crowds from the minaret.

End of April: Efes Kültür Festivalı. A folklore festival in the ancient theatre at Ephesus.

First week in May: Marmaris Yatcılık Festivalı international regatta.

End of May: Silifke Festivalı. Dancers dressed in colourful costumes perform in a folk dancing festival.

Mid-June: Marmaris Sanaat Festivalı. Concerts, plays, watersports competitions.

End of June: Çeşme Deniz Festivalı. Pop festival in Çeşme; Foça Müzik Festivalı.

Mid-August: Truva Festivalı. Folklore in Troy.

20 August–20 September: İzmir Fuarı. İzmir International Trade Fair with cultural events.

First week in September: Bodrum Festivalı. Artistic and cultural events.

Second week in October: Akdeniz Müzik Festivalı. Music festival in Antalya and wrestling in Aspendos.

Third week in October: Antalya Altın Portakal Festivalı. Turkish film festival.

6–8 December: Festival of St Nicholas in Kale/Demre.

Festive presentation

Food and Drink

Opposite: delivery man in İsparta

Modern Turkish cuisine unites the nomadic tradition with Arabic and Greek cooking. One of the most distinctive features is the wide variety of vegetable preparations. Along the west coast, dishes are only sparingly seasoned with mint, parsley or garlic (*sarmısak*). Many hotels and restaurants in the tourist regions have adjusted their menus to suit the palates of Western visitors, so in order to sample real Turkish fare, it will be necessary to take a trip to the basic *lokantalar*, a potentially rewarding experience.

Appetisers and soups

A rich and varied cuisine

It is often possible to choose appetisers (*mezeler*) straight from the buffet. Popular choices include fried liver cubes with onions (*arnavut ciğeri*), yoghurt with cucumber, dill and garlic (*cacik*), aubergine paste (*patlıcan kızartmazı*), chicken paste with nuts (*çerkez tavuğu*), bean salad (*piyaz*), hot tomato purée (*azme ezme*), chick pea purée (*humus*), filo pastry rolls with ewes' cheese (*sigara böreği*).

83

Soups (*çorbalar*), on the other hand, are only available in simple eating houses (*lokanta*). Lentil soup (*mercimek çorbası*), fish soup (*balık çorbası*), tripe soup (*işkembe çorbası*) or a rice soup with yoghurt and peppermint (*yala çorbası*) are frequently encountered.

Main courses

Tourist restaurants specialise in meat dishes and beef, lamb and chicken will always be on the menu, but Moslems are not allowed to eat pork. Spit-roasted *döner kebabs* are only available from *lokanta* as are *Adana kebab* (minced meat on a skewer), *köfte* (minced meatballs) and *Şişkebab* (lamb on a skewer).

At the coast the choice of fish and seafood dishes is wide and tempting. Octopus salad (*ahtapodi salada*), red mullet (*barbunya*), gilthead (*çupra*), sea perch (*levrek*), swordfish (*kılıç balığı*), red bream (*mercan*), prawns (*karides*) or lobster (*istakos*) are Mediterranean delicacies which are best eaten fresh. When choosing fish, look for clear eyes. If they are suffused with blood, then the fish has been out of the sea for too long and should be avoided.

A tempting array

Dolmalar, vegetables stuffed with rice and pine kernels, are a typical Turkish dish, and are usually served lukewarm.

Desserts

Melon surprise

In summer, fruit – perhaps honeydew melon (*kavun*), watermelon (*karpuz*), dessert grapes (*üzüm*) or oranges (*portakal*) – is nearly always served after the main course. If you require something a little sweeter, then try filo pastries with nuts and honey such as *baklava* or *bülbül yuvas*.

Drinks

A selection of juices

Although Turkey is an Islamic country, all the better restaurants (*restoran*) serve beer (*bira*) and wine (*Şarap*) with meals. While beers from the Efes brewery can be recommended, Turkish wine has little to commend it. Most Turks usually drink *ayran* (salty yoghurt thinned with water) with meals or else mineral water (*maden suyu*; drinking water in bottles is called *kaynak suyu*). Tea the national drink (*çay*) is first prepared as a strong brew and then diluted with hot water. In a good tea garden (*çay bahçesi*) guests can ask for a samovar (*çay samaver*). Each cup of Turkish mocca coffee (*kahve*) is brewed separately and then served with the grounds. *Rakı*, an aniseed spirit, is often drunk in the evenings. It too is rarely consumed neat but diluted with water, whereupon the otherwise clear liquid becomes cloudy. *Şerefe* is the Turkish equivalent of 'cheers'.

Restaurant selection

These suggestions for some of the most popular destinations are listed according to the following categories: $$$ = expensive; $$ = moderate; $ = inexpensive.

Alanya

Making bread in Alanya

$$$**Janus**, by the harbour. International-class restaurant. $$$**Halikarnos**, near the tower. Good fish dishes. Typically Turkish restaurants in the bazaar quarter, eg **Doyum** (large selection of starters $$) or **Gaziantep** (eastern Turkish specialities). In addition, there are simple *lokantalar* on Atatürk Cad. and towards the *dolmuş* station.

Adana

Adana is not an established centre for tourists so many of the restaurants are fairly basic with a good choice in Inönü Cad., Özler Cad. and Atatürk Bul.; snack bars in the bazaar quarter or near the station. The $$$ restaurant at the **Seyhan Hotel** is the best in the city.

Delicious baklavas

Antakya

$**Anadolu**, corner of Saray Cad. and Hürriyet Cad. Pretty garden restaurant. Basic snack bars, kebab stands and *lokantalar* in the picnic park at Harbiye.

Antalya

$$**Restoran Hisar**, in the fort beneath Cumhuriyet Meydanı. Fine view. $**Türk Evi Restoran**, Mermerli Sok. 2. by the steps to the harbour mosque, in a magnificently-renovated Ottoman house with attractive garden courtyard. There are many simple $ restaurants serving traditional Turkish fare in the covered **Eski Sebzeçiler Sokak** and in the parallel lane at the start of Atatürk Cad.

Assos/Behramkale
$$Athena Restaurant, Behramkale. Traditional Turkish fare and highly recommended. Reservation advisable.
$$Eden Beach, Kadırga. Fish and seafood specialities.
$Kervansaray, **Yıldız** and **Behram** hotels around Assos harbour all offer acceptable meals.

Ayvalık
$$Öz Canlı, Balık, Elif 2 and **Kanelo**, three decent restaurants in Ayvalık's Gazinolar Cad. Fish specialities. **$$Büyük Berk**, Sarımsaklı. Seafood in good hotel restaurant.

Bergama
$$Kardeşler Restaurant, İzmir Caddesi. Opposite the Archaeological Museum. Best restaurant in town. Basic **snack bars** on Bankalar Cad. and in the bazaar.

Bodrum
$$$Emin Fish Restaurant, Karantina Cad. 31. Wide range of starters, pleasant atmosphere. **$$$Han Restoran**, by the eastern bay with castle view. Excellent cuisine.

Çanakkale
$$Anafartalar, superb restaurant on hotel roof offering fine views. **$$Yeni Entellektüel**, Rıhtım Boyu 17, one of the best restaurants on the sea front.

Çeşme
The best **$$** fish and seafood restaurants are located in the Dalyanköy quarter to the north of the town, eg **Körfez Restaurant**, **Liman Restaurant**, **Dalyan Restaurant**, **Cinar Balık Restaurant**. The more modestly priced restaurants are situated near the harbour.

Fethiye
$$Rafet Restoran, by the harbour with fine sea view.
$$Zeki. One of the many good restaurants in the old town.

Güllübahce (Priene)
$Şelale Restaurant, Shady spot by a waterfall on the way to the ruins. Grilled trout a speciality.

İzmir
$$$Deniz Restauran, Atatürk Cad. 188. An exclusive restaurant serving the finest fish. **$$Bergama Restauran**, Atatürk Cad. 296. Livelier than the Deniz, good sea view and excellent fish. **$$Çiçek Passage**, Atatürk Cad. 132. Especially good mussels, young clientele. **$$Canli Balık**, Cumhuriyet Bulvarı 50. **$$Eighteen Eighty-Eight**, Cumhuriyet Bulvarı 248. **$$Halil**, Kibris Şehitleri Cad. 177/A. **$$Crystal**, Kibris Şehitleri Cad. 70/A.

Fresh fish

85

Restaurateur in Çanakkale

Kaş

$$$Mercan, by the harbour (on the left), idyllic spot at sunset. **$$Eriş**, by the square near the souvenir shops. Traditional restaurant serving Turkish fare. **$Orkinos**, in the row of restaurants between the centre of the harbour and market square. Decent fare, friendly proprietor.

Kızkalesi

Numerous traditionally Turkish restaurants, eg **$Kilikya** near the post office. Metre-long loaves fresh from the oven.

Kuşadası

The main roads for restaurants are Güvercin Ada Yolu, Atatürk Bulvarı (fish restaurants by the harbour), Kahramanlar Caddesi and Sağlık Caddesi in the town centre (good kebab snack bars).

Marmaris

A snack with substance

Most restaurants are situated on the promenade. Many offer fish specialities. The restaurants in the side streets are both quieter and cheaper.

Selçuk

With so many small restaurants in the alleys around the post office, at night the whole area is like one big open air dining hall. Plenty of atmosphere.

Side

Large choice by the harbour (**Afrodit, Mergiz**) and on both coastal promenades. **$$Soundwaves**, on the eastern promenade. Popular steak restaurant, always full.

Silifke

Lots of squashes

$Kale Restoran, on the castle terrace. Good view.

Active Holidays

Walking

The extensive, almost uninhabited mountain region behind the Mediterranean coast makes fascinating walking country. Particularly recommended are the remote high plains around Kozak (north of Bergama), the woodland near Bodrum and Marmaris and also the Yaylas above Alanya. In the Lycian part of the Taurus mountains it is even possible to stumble upon undiscovered ancient remains. Spring and autumn when it is not too hot are unquestionably the best times of year for walking tours. Always wear sturdy shoes and carry a good supply of water and some nourishing food for emergencies. Detailed maps are not available, so a compass is essential. Otherwise, call upon the services of a local guide.

A local guide

Canoeing

Many of the wild mountain streams that flow down the sides of the Taurus mountains are ideal for canoeing. There are a number of new companies which hire out equipment and also arrange for transport to the destination. One of the rivers much favoured by canoeing enthusiasts is the Göksu Canyon, just north of Side.

Watersports

Water skiing off the main tourist resorts is very popular and the charges are reasonable. Given the strong breezes that blow at Çeşme and Bodrum, both these resorts are popular with windsurfers. Equipment is available for hire.

Windsurfing boards for hire

Diving

The bays and rocky coastline of the Aegean, the Lycian coast and near Kızkalesı offer divers a wide variety of underwater conditions. Lucky divers might even find some ancient remains and it is for this reason that unaccompanied scuba diving is not encouraged and problems can sometimes arise with the police. Any finds must be handed over. Equipment may be hired in Bodrum, Marmaris, Kaş, Kızkalesı and many other resorts. Lessons and guided underwater expeditions to places of interest are also offered. **Snorkelling** is a good alternative almost everywhere.

Many resorts offer day trips

Boat trips

The 'Blue Trip' yacht cruise as it is known has an almost magical reputation. Boats leave Bodrum and follow the Aegean coast as far as Kaş, passing from one blue-shimmering bay to the next. These trips can be booked from travel agents at home. Other smaller boat trips leave from Kuşadası, Bodrum, Marmaris and Fethiye. Ask for details at the local tourist offices. Many resorts offer day trips.

Getting There

By air

Charter flights to the Turkish Mediterranean coast are available all the year round and it is worth making a comparison between fares, as bargains are often available from the smaller tour operators. Visitors who do not wish to make firm hotel bookings can reserve a place on a 'camping flight'. Turkish Airlines (THY) operates regular scheduled flights to Izmir, Antalya, Dalaman and Adana from most major cities. Contact a THY office for information, reservations and discounts:

In the UK: 11–12 Hanover Street, London W1R 9HF, tel: 0171-499 4499; fax: 0171-495 2441.

In the US: 437 Madison Avenue, New York, NY 10022, tel: 212-339 9650; fax: 212-339 9680. 5230 Pacific Concourse Drive, Suite 200, Los Angeles, Ca 90045, tel: 310-643 4595; fax: 310-643 4499.

Parking in Ayvalık

89

Overland

It is still relatively easy to get to Turkey by car but it is best to avoid the former Yugoslavian route. Get the ferry to Belgium and drive through Germany to Vienna, then to Budapest, on to Bucharest through Romania and to Burgas in Bulgaria and into Turkey and İstanbul. If you want to go by sea for some of the route, car ferries to Turkey leave from Italy (Brindisi and Venice) and Igoumenitsa (Greece).

There are no special formalities required for car drivers but vehicle details will be entered in the driver's passport. A national driving licence will be required, together with vehicle registration documents and nationality disc. Obtain an International Green Card from your insurance company and ensure that the certificate is valid for the Asian part of Turkey. Fully-comprehensive travel insurance is recommended. A vehicle can be brought into Turkey for up to 6 months.

Turkey has an extensive network of well maintained roads linking her towns and cities. When coming from Europe, the crossing of the Bosphorus to Asia has been facilitated by the completion of the İstanbul bypass.

By sea

Ferries offer a safer and more relaxing route to Turkey, particularly for those who wish to take their own vehicle. Between May and October Turkish Maritime Lines operate a twice-weekly car ferry service from Venice to Kuşadası and Antalya. Ferries run by Çeşme Lines ply between Brindisi and Çeşme on a twice-weekly basis. Contact the shipping lines through Sunquest, 23 Princes St, London W1R 7RG, tel: 0171-499 9992.

Yeni Foça harbour

İzmir station

Getting Around

By air

Almost all of the larger towns have an airport nearby, but nearly all the domestic flights operated by Türk Hava Yolları (THY), the national Turkish airline company, link the provincial centres with İstanbul or Ankara. So change in İstanbul to fly from İzmir to Antalya and in Ankara if flying from Antalya to Adana.

By rail

The wide network of Turkish State Railways connects most major cities. The trains have couchettes, sleeping-cars and restaurants, with lounge cars offering first and second class service. However, the efficiency of Turkish railways is surpassed both in speed and comfort by the bus services. Trains do not run along the main section of the Mediterranean coast between Selçuk and Mersin, although in the Aegean region it is possible for groups to charter a steam train over a route of their choice. For further information contact a Turkish tourist information office.

By bus

The bus is by far the most important form of public transport. Long-distance bus services link all the major towns along the coast at almost hourly intervals. Services are good, though not necessarily for the faint hearted. Tickets are issued by the company offices at the bus stations (*otogar*) and these also guarantee a seat. To avoid queueing, it is possible to pay during the journey. At religious festivals, it is advisable to book well in advance.

Taxis and dolmuş

Compared to European taxis, the Turkish yellow taxis are very cheap. In the towns, fares are calculated from the taximeter, but for longer journeys, tariffs are laid down by the government. It is also possible to hire a taxi for a day with prices based roughly on the cost of a hire car.

The *dolmuş*, a special service unique to Turkey, is a collective taxi which follows specific routes and is recognisable by its yellow band. Each passenger pays according to the distance travelled and can get off at specific stops. The cheap fares are fixed by the municipality. The *dolmuş* provides a service within large cities to suburbs, airports and often to neighbouring towns and the more remote rural regions. The destination is shown on the windscreen and a hand signal is all that is needed to stop a *dolmuş*.

Vehicle hire

Car hire companies are based in all the main resorts. International agencies such as Europcar, Avis and Hertz

Scooters for hire

are generally more expensive than the local companies, but then they usually provide a better emergency service. Prices range from £30 per day for a small car to £60 for a jeep. When booking a car, driving licence and passport must be produced. Minimum age is 21. Before driving off, check that the car has a spare tyre and jack. On the main trunk roads petrol stations are usually open for 24 hours even on Sunday.

Traffic

The road network by the coast is good, but away from the main centres of population in the mountain regions drivers should be prepared for narrow, winding and unsecured tracks. Use first gear and brake with the engine when making steep descents; take particular care on bends. Herds of goats and other animals occasionally block the way. At night and at dusk, many local cars use sidelights instead of headlights and donkey carts do not carry any lights at all. Turkish drivers can be rather unpredictable but, apart from bus and lorry drivers, they are generally defensive rather than aggressive. Turkish drivers often sound their horns to warn that they are about to overtake. In the event of an accident, the police must be informed and an alcohol test taken, otherwise the Turkish insurance companies will not pay up. When a driver, passenger or pedestrian is injured, it is advisable to seek legal assistance. The US and British embassies (or consulates) can provide the addresses of English-speaking lawyers.

The following telephone numbers may be useful in the event of an accident or breakdown:

Türkiye Turing ve Otomobil Kurumu, İzmir, tel: 232/422 2621; Antalya, tel: 242/247 0699; Mersin, tel: 324/232 0492; İskenderun, tel: 326/617 7462.

There are numerous repair garages in towns and along principal highways. Spare parts are readily available. Turkish mechanics are well trained in the repair of both Turkish and foreign cars. Filling stations are well distributed along all roads, and those on the main highways often have attached service stations and restaurants, and are open around the clock.

Traffic regulations

The maximum permitted speed in towns is 50kmph (31mph), on trunk roads 90kmph (56mph). Radar controls are rare, but are sometimes used, particularly on the busy roads leading out of main towns. Seat belts must be worn and driving after drinking alcohol is forbidden. Anyone found with traces of alcohol in their blood can expect a hefty punishment. Turkish road signs are similar to European signs. Archaeological and historical sites are indicated by yellow signs.

Catering to all needs

91

Spare parts are readily available

The city gate at Side

Alternative transport

*Most resorts have
information offices*

Facts for the Visitor

Travel documents

Nationals of the United Kingdom and the US require a visa to enter Turkey for a period of up to three months. Visas are issued upon entering the country, so there is no need to apply for one in advance. Travellers from other countries are advised to contact the Turkish Embassy before leaving home.

Customs

Carpets may be exported only if a receipt giving the age of the carpet can be produced. The export of antiques (pre-1945) is forbidden. Under Turkish regulations, only 200 cigarettes and 1 litre of spirits above 22 percent may be imported.

Tourist information

Visitors requiring more information about Turkey prior to departure should contact the Turkish Tourist Office in their home country.

In the UK: First Floor, 170–173 Piccadilly, London W1V 9DD, tel: (0171) 355 4207, fax: (0171) 491 0733.

In the US: 821 United Nations Plaza, New York, NY 10017, tel: (212) 687 2194/5/6, fax: (212) 599 7568; 1717 Massachusetts Avenue NW Suite 306, Washington DC, tel: (202) 429 9844, fax: (202) 429 5649.

In Turkey

Tourist information offices can be found in most resorts on the coast. Although the staff are generally very willing to help, the offices are not always well supplied with leaflets, brochures, etc. Opening times are usually 9am–noon and 2–6pm, often later in the evening.

Tourist information offices in the resorts

İzmir: Adnan Menderes airport, tel: 232/251 2626; on the Gazi Osmanpaşa Bulvarı (ground floor of the Grand Hotel Efes), tel: 232/484 2147; Atatürk Cad. 418, tel: 232/421 6841. **Çeşme:** İskele Meydanı 8, by the harbour, tel: 232/892 1328. A list of hotels and pensions is available here. **Antalya:** Cumhuriyet Ca. 91, tel: 242/247 6298 and by the harbour, tel: 242/247 0541. **Çanakkale:** İskele Meydanı 67, by the ferry port, tel: 286/217 1187. **Ayvalık:** Yat Limani Karsısı, tel: 266/312 2122. **Bergama:** İzmir Cad. 54, tel: 232/633 1862. **Selçuk:** Agora Carsısı, tel: 232/612 1130. **Kuşadası:** İskele Meydanı, tel: 256/614 1103. **Bodrum:** Eylül Meydanı, tel: 252/316 1091. **Marmaris**: İskele Meydanı 2, tel: 252/412 1035. **Köyceğiz**: tourist office, by the harbour, tel: 252/262 4703. **Fethiye**: tourist office, by the harbour, tel: 252/614 1527. **Kaş**: tourist office, by the harbour square, tel: 242/836 1238. **Kemer**: tourist office, by the harbour, tel: 242/814 1536. **Side**: tourist office, by the bus station outside the town gate, tel: 242/753 1265. **Alanya**: tourist office in Damlataş Cad., tel: 242/513 1240. **Anamur**: tourist office, Bulvar Cad. 42B, tel: 324/814 3529. **Silifke**: tourist office, Veli Bozbey Cad. 6, tel: 324/714 1151. **Adana**: tourist office, Atatürk Cad. 13, tel: 322/359 1994. **Antakya**: tourist office, Vali Ürgen Alanı 47, tel: 326/216 0610.

Currency and exchange

The currency of Turkey is the Turkish lira. Bank notes in circulation are for 5,000, 10,000, 20,000, 50,000, 100,000, 250,000, 500,000 and 1,000,000TL. With inflation currently running at about 150 percent, it is impossible to give an indication of exchange rates. There is no limit to the amount of foreign currency which may be imported, but amounts greater than the equivalent of US$ 5,000 must be declared on entry. It is advisable to change only small amounts of Turkish lira at home, as the exchange rates there are likely to be unfavourable. In western Turkey cash, travellers' cheques and sterling Eurocheques can be exchanged at banks, post offices, travel agents and hotels. Eurocheques may not be so welcome in eastern Turkey. Only the larger hotels and car hire firms in the west of the country will accept credit cards.

Opening times

Shops open from Monday to Saturday 8.30am–7pm, but for longer and on Sunday in the main resorts. Offices are open from Monday to Friday 9am–noon and 1.30–5.30pm but, by the Mediterranean coast, most close in the afternoon. During Şeker Bayramı and Kurban Bayramı (*see page 94*), both festivals which can last for several days, offices often close for the whole week. Most Turkish mu-

93

Antique carpets for sale

seums are open every day of the week, except Mondays. Palaces are also closed only on Mondays.

Public holidays

National holidays: 1 January (New Year's Day); 23 April (Children's Day); 19 May (Youth Day); 30 August (Victory Day); 29 October (Republic Day).

Religious festivals

The dates for Şeker Bayramı and Kurban Bayramı are calculated by the Islamic calendar and will change from year to year. Banks, museums and most shops will be closed on these dates.

A wide choice of souvenirs

Shopping and souvenirs

The choice of souvenirs is very wide. Hand-made brass and copper goods, finely carved woodwork, meerschaum pipes and plates with Islamic motifs are often produced according to traditional Ottoman designs.

Copper pots

Vases and jars of alabaster and onyx or jewellery made from gold and semi-precious stones are available in more modern styles. Herbs, spices, honeys and jams are easy to find in the bazaars. When it comes to carpets and kilims, it is a case of *caveat emptor* (*see page 13*). Leather goods are excellent value. It is perfectly acceptable to haggle and you can expect to be able to reduce the first price quoted by about a third.

Postal services

Post office sign

General post offices (*postahane, PTT*) in the main towns are usually open from Monday to Saturday 8am–midnight, Sunday 9am–7pm. They can be recognised by their yellow signs. The smaller offices open Monday to Sunday 8am–12.30pm and 1.30–5.30pm, or for longer in the tourist centres.

Cash, travellers' cheques and Eurocheques can all be exchanged at post offices. An express postal service (APS) operates from Turkey to 72 other countries for letters, documents and small packages. Stamp collectors will be delighted and amazed by the wide range of special stamps available to them.

Telephone

Tokens or phonecards (available from post offices) are needed to make calls from phone boxes, but it is often simpler to use the phones at the counters in the post offices.

To make an overseas call, dial 00 followed by the international code (UK 44; US and Canada 1) followed by the local code (omitting the initial zero from numbers in the UK) and the subscriber's number. The international code for Turkey is 0090.

Time

Turkey observes Eastern European Time which is two hours ahead of GMT. Turkish Summer Time (beginning of April to the end of September) is three hours ahead of GMT.

Clothing

Loose cottons are recommended for the summer, but not shorts or strapless or low-cut sun-dresses. The Turks place great emphasis on correct clothing. In spring and autumn, and if planning trips into the mountains, do not forget to pack a warm pullover and an anorak. Sturdy shoes are essential at many of the archaeological sites and bathing sandals are advisable for negotiating the stony bays on the west coast.

Nudism

Nude bathing is strictly forbidden. Even in the holiday villages, topless bathing may well be misunderstood by young men.

Photography

Films are available in Turkey but expensive. Taking photographs of military installations is forbidden and before filming or photographing individuals, a gesture requesting permission is usually appreciated.

Medical assistance

Medical provision in Turkey is no worse than in many other European countries, but doctors practise mainly in the bigger towns. Chemists (*eczane,* 8.30am–7pm) have many medications available without prescriptions.

Emergency numbers: chemist 119; doctor 112.

Medical precautions and insurance

Vaccinations are not officially required, but it is advisable to obtain an anti-tetanus booster. A slight risk of malaria exists in the Çukorova plain between March and November, so it may be worthwhile taking the necessary precautions. Given the intensity of the Mediterranean sun in summer, take good supplies of a high-factor sun cream. Avoid very oily dishes during the first few days.

All visitors should take out a private holiday insurance policy to cover every eventuality. Medical treatment is provided under the Turkish social security system (*Sosyal Sigortalar Kumuru*).

Crime

Property crimes are rare in Turkey, except in the main cities; however, it is not uncommon for taxi-drivers, bazaar salesmen and café owners to take advantage of tourists. In

Don't be afraid to haggle

blatant cases, contact the police, tel: 155 in all areas, or the local tourist police.

Beware of touts

In some resorts touts, usually friendly young men, are becoming a nuisance. They work on a commission basis and their job is to entice as many customers as possible into the carpet warehouse to buy a souvenir carpet. They know all the tricks but usually a good-natured remark is all that is needed to send them off.

Beggars

Beggars and cripples can be seen everywhere in Turkey. They obtain no state aid and live in desperate poverty, although many of them receive help from the mosque as one of the duties for Moslems is to give alms to the poor. Do not give child beggars money. Some parents send their children out to beg instead of sending them to school.

Return of VAT

VAT at 15 percent was introduced in 1994. In order to claim this back, receipts should be retained and produced when leaving the country. When purchasing expensive goods such as carpets, establish whether VAT is included in the price, before asking for a receipt.

Diplomatic representation

Symbolic of Turkey

Embassies in Ankara
United Kingdom: Sehit Ersan Cad, 46/A, Cankaya, tel: 312-468 6230.
United States of America: Atatürk Bulv, 110, Kavaklidere, tel: 312-468 6110-28.

Consulates
United Kingdom:
Anatalya: Kızılsaray Mah, Dolaplıdere Cad, Pırıltı Sitesi, Kat 1, tel: 242-247 7000.
Bodrum: Atatürk Cad, Adilye Sokak 12/C, tel: 252-316 4932.
Iskenderun: Catoni Maritime Agency, Maresal Cakmak Cad 28/D, tel: 326-613 0361-64.
İstanbul: Mesrutiyet Cad 34, Beyoglu/Tepebasi, tel: 212-293 7540.
İzmir: 1442 Sokak 49, Alsancak, tel: 232-463 5151.
Mersin: Çakmak Cad 124, Sokak, M Tece is Merkezi, A Blok, Kat 4, No 4, tel: 324-232 1248/237 8687.
United States of America:
Adana: Atatürk Cad, Vali olu, tel: 322-453 9106.
İzmir: Amerikan Kültür Dernegi, Kat 2, tel: 232-421 3643.
İstanbul: Mesrutiyet Cad 104–108, Tepebasi, tel: 212-251 3602.

Slippers for sale at Çeşme

Accommodation

97

Hotels of every category have been built during the last few years, so independent travellers can usually find somewhere that suits their pocket. It is normal to ask to see the room and prices are agreed on the spot. Visitors who are not on a package tour should not book their hotel from home as they will find themselves paying for the reductions and discounts offered to the main tour operators.

Hotels

Most of the newer hotels provide good quality accommodation and at very reasonable prices. Even in the lower categories, all rooms have a shower and toilet. When the prices rise above $40, then expect to find a swimming pool with bar. Rooms priced from $50 will probably have air conditioning. Many internationally-owned and luxury hotels calculate their room prices in dollars (from $80). Breakfast (European or Turkish) is normally included in the price.

Pensions

A room in a smallish family-run pension (*pansiyon*) can cost from as little as $10, but as a rule such rooms are best avoided in the large towns.

Clubs

Traditional club in Manavgat

Large and well-equipped clubs near Foça, Kuşadası, Bodrum, Marmaris, Fethiye, Side and Kemer can offer a wide range of sporting and leisure activities and they also organise excursions.

Camping

Camp-sites are usually situated close to the main trunk roads and some also offer motel-style accommodation.

From the comfort point of view they have little to commend them, certainly not in summer, as the temperature in a tent, caravan or wood cabin can rise to over 60°C (140°F).

Apartments at İskenderun

Hotel selection

The following are hotel suggestions for some of the destinations. Here they appear in three categories: $$$ = expensive; $$ = moderate; $ = inexpensive.

Adana

$$$Seyhan Oteli, Turkan Cenmal Beriker Bulv. 30, tel: 322/475 8101, fax: 454 2834. On the main thoroughfare, high standard of comfort, swimming pool. **$$Hosta Hotel**, Bakımyurdu Cad. 3, 322/352 3700. Reasonably-priced inner-city hotel, mainly used by business people. **$$Duygu Oteli**, İnönü Cad. 14, tel: 322/359 3916. Basic hotel.

Alanya hotels

Alanya

$$$Hotel Bedesten, tel: 242/512 1234, fax: 513 7934. Luxury hotel in converted caravanserai, on the citadel. **$$Kaptan Otel**, İskele Cad., tel: 242/513 2000. Modern hotel with small swimming pool, above the harbour. **$$Sultan Otel**, Damlataş Cad., tel: 242/513 1348. Near Cleopatra beach. Modern hotel with swimming pool and lawn. **$$Wien Otel**, Keykubat Cad., tel: 242/513 3617. Separated from the eastern beach by the road. Basic and rather noisy.

Altınkum (*Didyma*)

$$$Hotel Kardelen, Altınkum, tel: 0356/813 3157. Modern hotel by the 'golden beach' (4km/2½ miles).

Anamur

$$Hotel Anahan, Tahsin Soylu Cad., tel: 324/8 4 3512. Older hotel, but with large rooms. Open all the year round. **$$Meltem Otel**, in İskele by the beach, tel: 324/8 4 2316. Modern hotel with restaurant. Many more hotels and pensions in İskele, and also to the east of Mamure Kalesi.

Antakya

$$$Büyük Antakya Oteli, Atatürk Cad. 8, tel: 326/213 5860, fax: 213 5869. Best hotel in town. European-standard restaurant. **$$Defay Oteli**, Defne Cad., tel: 326/231 4054. Newish hotel on the edge of town.

Antalya

$$$Aspen Oteli, Kaledibi Lok. 16, tel: 242/247 0590. Pure luxury in a renovated town house. **$$Argos**, Balıkpazarı Sok., tel: 242/247 2012. In the old town. Swimming pool, sauna, garden restaurant. **$$Frankfurt Pansiyon**, Hıdırlık

Sok. 17, tel: 242/247 6224. Family-run hotel in the old town. **$Hadrianus Pansiyon**, Zeytin Çikmazı, tel: 242/241 2313. Simple rooms with shower, garden.

Assos/Behramkale

$$Assos Kervansaray, by the marina, tel: 286/712 7199. Renovated caravanserai. **$Behram Oteli**, by the harbour, tel: 286/712 7016. Restaurant. Several pensions by the harbour and also in the village of Behramkale, for those who do not mind basic accommodation (**İnci Pansiyon, Mustafa Pansiyon**). **$Eden Beach Motel**, by Kadırga Beach, tel: 286/712 2017. Good restaurant.

Ayvalık

$$$Grand Temizel Oteli, Sarımsaklı, tel: 266/324 2000. Comfortable hotel by the main square. **$$Murat Reis**, Sarımsaklı, tel: 266/324 1456. Older, high-class hotel by a small bay. Swimming pool, disco, restaurant. **$$Büyük Berk**, Sarımsaklı, tel: 266/324 1045. Well maintained hotel with swimming pool and disco. **$Aytur Motel**, Alibey Adası, tel: 266/327 1014. Pleasant location by the sea. Basic rooms. Pensions and camp-sites can be found in Sarımsaklı and Alibey.

Bergama

$$Tusan Motel, tel: 232/633 1173. 7km (4 miles) from the town by the junction of the motorway and the road to Bergama. Shielded from the traffic noise by trees. Rooms with balconies, restaurant. **$$İskender Oteli**, İzmir Cad., tel: 232/633 2123. Older hotel in the town, rather noisy. **$$Yıldır Oteli**, tel: 232/633 3084. Diagonally opposite the post office on the edge of the bazaar. Opened in 1993. Unexceptional service but the best place in town.

Bodrum

$$Monastir Hotel, Bariş Sitesi, tel: 252/316 2858. On the outskirts, but in a pleasant, peaceful spot overlooking the bay. Swimming pool and tennis court. **$$Hotel Maya**, Gerence Sok. 49, tel: 252/316 4741. Quiet and comfortable. Swimming pool and air conditioning. **$Baraz Oteli**, Hilmi Uran Cad., near the Cumhuriyet Cad., tel: 252/316 1857. Old town hotel by the bay at the east end of town.

Çanakkale

$$$Akol Oteli, Kayserili Ahmet Paşa Cad., tel: 286/217 9456. Most comfortable hotel in town. **$$Hotel Anafartalar**, İskele Meydanı (by the Dardanelles), tel: 286/217 4455. Comfortable town hotel. Rooms overlooking the sea with balcony, but noisy. **$$Hotel Büyük Truva**, Yalıboyu Cad., tel: 286/217 4811. Further away from the ferry terminal and a bit quieter. Not so well furnished.

Bergama from Pergamon

Çeşme

$$$Framissima Boyalık Beach Hotel, Boyalık, tel: 232/712 7081, fax: 712 7331. By the beach. Çeşme's most luxurious hotel. **$$Kanun Kervanseray**, Çeşme Kalesi Yani, tel: 232/712 7177, fax: 712 6492. Romantic hotel in a 16th-century caravanserai near the harbour. Pretty inner courtyard with fountain. Good rooms. **$$Hotel Hora**, Ilıca, PTT Yanı (near the post office), tel: 232/723 2654. Well-run hotel. **$Çeşme Marin Hotel**, Hürriyet Cad. 10, tel: 232/712 7579. Smallish but pleasant hotel on the sea front.

Fethiye

$$$Club Letoonia, situated on a headland in the west of the town (6km/4 miles), tel: 252/614 4966, fax: 614 4422. Modern complex, air conditioned rooms, watersports, swimming pool, sauna, disco. **$$Dedeoğlu Oteli**, tel: 252/614 4010. Opposite the jetty to the west of the old town. Pleasant town hotel within easy reach of the centre. **$$Levent Oteli**, Kasagözler Fevzi Çakmak Cad. 2, tel: 252/614 5873. On the coast road behind the harbour, about 10 minutes from the town centre. Friendly, family-run hotel with swimming pool. Many hotels and pensions are situated by the long Çalış beach, 4km (2½ miles) to the north. There are plenty of watersports facilities in the area.

İzmir

$$$Hilton, Gazi Osmanpaşa Bulvarı 7, tel: 232/441 6060, fax: 441 2277. The best hotel in the city. Central location. **$$$Grand Hotel Efes**, Gazi Osmanpaşa Bulvarı 1, tel: 232/484 4300, fax: 441 5695. Oldest luxury hotel in the city, with pool bar, terrace restaurant and casino. **$$$İzmir Etap**, Cumhuriyet Bulvarı 138, tel: 232/489

İzmir from the citadel

Popular Pamukkale

4090, fax: 480 4089. Luxury hotel but half the price of the Hilton and the Efes. **$$Otel Kısmet**, 1377 Sok. 9, tel: 232/463 3850. Enjoys a quiet, favourable location on the edge of the Alsancak district. Very good restaurant, bar and café. **$$Otel Yumukoğlu**, 1371 Sok. 8, tel: 232/413 6565. New and well-managed hotel near the Culture Park. **$Otel Kabacam**, 1364 Sok. 2/1, tel: 232/414 0549. In a quiet side street near the station. Small rooms. **$Otel Bayburt**, 1360 Sok. 1, tel: 232/412 2013. Older hotel, rather spartan, but clean and cheap.

Kalkan

$$$Hotel Pirat, by the harbour, tel: 242/844 3178, fax: 844 3183. Recently renovated and now the finest hotel on this section of coast. High-level of comfort in Greek neoclassical island style. Swimming pool, restaurant, watersports. **$$Balıkçıhan**, above the harbour, tel: 242/844 3075. Pension with bar and roof terrace. **$Akın**, near the Balıkçıhan, tel: 242/844 3162. Simple rooms in a fine Greek-style house.

Kaş

$$Kaş Hotel,on the street from the harbour to the theatre, tel: 242/836 1271. Villa-style complex with most rooms enjoying a sea view. Sunshades by the sea, and a nice restaurant. **$$Medusa Oteli**, on the street from the bus station to the harbour, tel: 242/836 1440. Older-style medium-category hotel with scuba diving facilities. **$Limyra Pansiyon**, on the right behind the Medusa, tel: 242/836 1716. Newish pension with attractive roof terrace and pleasant rooms.

Kemer

$$$Otem Hotel, by the harbour, tel: 242/814 3181, fax: 814 3190. One of the best hotels in the town, with swimming pool, spacious rooms and a variety of organised watersports. **$$$Kaftan Hotel**, Hastane Cad., 10P. Sok., on the edge of town out towards Çamyuva, tel: 242/814 4434, fax: 814 4435. A modern hotel, with swimming pool. **$$Jest Hotel**, situated on the left-hand side of the main road to Çamyuva, tel: 242/814 4868. Smaller hotel with a pleasant atmosphere.

Kızkalesi

$$$Club Barbarossa, Kızkalesi Mev., tel: 324/523 2364, fax: 523 2090. Luxury hotel with excellent restaurant and many other facilities. **$$Kilikya**, Kızkalesi Kesabası, tel: 324/523 2167. Good medium-category hotel. **$Başar Motel**, tel: 324/523 2035. Basic hotel, but friendly proprietor. Diving school. More hotels and many good value pensions nearby.

Köyceğiz
$$Özay Oteli, near the main square, tel: 252/262 4300.
Turkish furnishings.

Kuşadası
$$$Club Caravansérail, by the harbour, tel: 256/614
4115, fax: 614 2423. Luxury hotel in an Ottoman cara-
vanserai, beautifully renovated in Turkish style. **$$$Ho-
tel İmbat**, Kadınlar Denizi, tel: 256/614 2000, fax: 614
4960. A long-established hotel which has been modernised
a number of times. Pleasant restaurant and private beach.
$$Hotel Martı, Kadınlar Denizi, tel: 256/614 3650. Traditional hotel by Kadınlar beach. **$$Alp Oteli**, Yat Limanı
Karsısı, tel: 256/6 4 1512. Pleasant spot by the harbour.

Marmaris
$$$Altınyunus Hotel, Pamucak Mev., tel: 252/412 3617.
Luxury hotel with every possible amenity. Night-club and
casino. **$$Hotel Begonya**, tel: 252/412 4095. Well-ren-
ovated old town hotel behind the castle. **$Hotel Yavuz**,
Atatürk Cad. 59, tel: 252/412 2937/38. Town hotel with
baths and Ottoman atmosphere. Reasonably-priced apart-
ments on the outskirts along the road to Datça.

Milas (Labranda)
$$$Labranda Corinthia Hotel, tel: 252/522 2911, fax:
522 2009. Luxurious centre with swimming pool, fitness
room, tennis court, watersports, belly dancing evenings.

Selçuk
$$$Otel Tamsa, Pamucak, Corak, tel: 232/892 6190, fax:
892 2771. Modern, comfortable beach hotel, 9km (5 miles)
from Selçuk, 7km (4 miles) from Ephesus. **$$Otel Pınar**,
Şahabettin Dede Cad. tel: 232/892 2561. Pleasant rooms
with air conditioning. **$Otel Victoria**, Cengiz Topel Cad.
4, tel: 232/892 3203. Quiet location.

Side
$$$Kleopatra Hotel, on the village's west coast, tel:
242/753 1033, fax: 753 3738. High level of comfort. **$$Be-
len Hotel**, in the village near the east coast, tel: 242/753
1043. Family-run business. **$$Motel Sur**, by the harbour
in the village, tel: 242/753 1087. Good value, but noisy.
Accommodation of all categories in **Kumköy** to the west.

Silifke
Look for hotels in Taşucu or better ones in Kızkalesi.

Ulucınar
$$Arsuz, tel: 326/643 2444. The best accommodation
in the area.

Index